17 Days Left

By

Michael J May

Part IV of the 17 Days Series

Contents

Intro.	2
Day 1, Sunday, 10th of June.	3
Day 2, Monday, 11th of June.	23
Day 3, Tuesday, 12th of June.	35
Day 4, Wednesday, 13th of June.	45
Day 5, Thursday, 14th of June.	56
Day 6, Friday, 15th of June.	71
Day 7, Saturday, 16th of June.	86
Day 8, Sunday, 17th of June.	106
Day 9, Monday, 18th of June.	113
Day 10, Tuesday, 19th of June.	132
Day 11, Wednesday, 20th of June.	143
Day 12, Thursday, 21st of June.	157
Day 13, Friday, 22nd of June.	171
Day 14, Saturday, 23rd of June.	190
Day 15, Sunday, 24th of June.	204
Day 16, Monday, 25th of June.	216
Day 17, Tuesday, 26th of June.	226
Outro.	237
Acknowledgements.	238
My Writing Journey.	239
Loyalty and Honour; Chapter 1. The Hospital.	243

Intro.

A lot had changed a lot since 18 April. Jack had moved into his new office, Steve was all settled in his new café, his bar was done. All good. Nothing bad? Well, ok, Helen had moved away with the kids. When I say away, I mean to Huntingdon. May as well be on the other side of the country though as far as Jack was concerned. The kids had gotten used to their new routine, though James' dissatisfaction was growing. Living further away also meant less time spent with their dad. Something Jack was really struggling with. As were the kids.

As discussed in previous parts of this series, the Jack/Christelle relationship thus far had been devoid of sexual activity. They both had their issues to work through, and had agreed not to until they were both ready. There was a lot of tension throughout this period, and it was building steadily. It was getting tougher to abstain, for both of them, and Jack had a feeling that Florence would be the time and the place. Not only for THAT, but also for something else…

They'd decided to move the trip, so it was going to be before the family holiday in Greece. Chrissy and Jack had been together for almost 5 months now, and this was their first holiday together (I don't class the London trip as a holiday). They say you never really know someone until you go on holiday with them. Let's see how it goes.

Florence was only 16 days away…

Day 1, Sunday, 10th of June.

Day one finds our reluctant hero Jack feeling quite good about life in general; his mental health had been getting better. He has had a few appointments with his counselor, and enjoyed each and every visit. Things with Helen had steadied a bit, however Chrissy still hated her, and he still disliked her intently. She'd completed her move away from Ramsey, which still didn't sit well with anybody. Except Helen and whatever his name is of course. The financial toll was starting to get less; new clients had made things a lot better, and moving to the former Willow Tree Café office had worked miracles. He had been able to take on a part time editing assistant, Kyle, who was in his final year of a related degree course at Uni Centre Peterborough. He was 21, and extremely talented. The kids were doing fine for the most part; no issues at school, and they seemed ok with the whole divorce thing now. They had just accepted the routine. Following the move, James' increasing discontent was of growing concern, but Elsie was harder to read. *Hey, what about me?* Oh yeah, inner voice was still around, though mostly in a positive way these days. *You say the nicest things.*
Anyway, enough catch-up, let's get on with it...

I could hear the alarm somewhere in the distance, but my mind didn't seem ready to acknowledge it. Yesterday had been a long, busy day; Kyle and I had worked overtime to try get the week's work done. I was mentally exhausted. So, I know what you're thinking: *Hey, what now? You worked on a Saturday? Where are the kids?* Good questions. Worked on Saturday as we had a LOT of work that week.
So much, we couldn't finish it all by Friday.

I had contacted all the clients, and found a few that were willing to postpone their posts until Sunday morning.
That bought us Saturday. Hence we worked flat out to get it all done. The kids were away at their Aunts for the weekend, so it all worked out just right. Happy? Can we get back to the story now? Good.
Waking up was a struggle. Probably because I knew I had a busy day ahead; I was throwing a bbq party tomorrow, and (in my head at least) had a lot of stuff to do to make it happen. Slowly, I opened my eyes and reached over to silence the insistent noise coming from my phone. Ever increasing in volume, it was starting to do my head in. It was only 06.30, and super bright already. Chrissy was still asleep next to me, oblivious of the alarm. I carefully got out, and changed into running gear. The weather had been fantastic; sunshine all day, maxing out at about 24C. Bliss. This morning, there was still a bit of a chill in the air, chill being relative. Once you get used to mid-20's weather, 12 degrees feels chilly. I walked along to the bridge as my watch located satellites. Eventually, it beeped, and I was ready to get started. I pushed start and trotted off down the tow path. It was beautiful out; bees were buzzing about, birds were singing, and the few people I saw all looked happy. Summer really had a magical effect on nature and humanity. I had been running the same route for a few years now, but I never tired of it. 5K is not a long distance (relatively), so it didn't really matter where I did it; here as good a place as any. There was always something to see; be it a heron, some geese, the usual swans, flowers, just anything really. I loved it. I couldn't ever envisage myself living anywhere else.

I ran past the spot where I first met the love of my life. It seemed like a lifetime ago, but was only 5 months. I could still see her running out from the trees, desperately trying to catch up with Chico, who had just escaped.

I fell for her immediately. Sounds silly saying it, but I did.
She was the most beautiful woman I'd ever met, and turned out to be the most perfect one too.
My kids loved her too, which was a massive bonus; we fitted together perfectly. We were all looking forward to our upcoming holiday in Greece, it was going to be awesome.
I made it back to the bridge, stopped my watch, and did a bit of stretching. I was sweating hard; it was muggy already. I don't do well in the heat, more of a cold weather person. I made my way back and jumped in the shower. I enjoyed the cool water for as long as I could stand it, then got out. Once I'd dried off, I crept back into the bedroom, got some clothes out, and got dressed.
"I can think of worse ways to wake up" I heard from behind me. Made me jump.
"Jesus, how long you been awake?" I asked.
"Long enough" she said, and gave a theatrical wink. *Whoa! She saw you naked! Get in!*
"You want coffee?" I said, throwing my towel at her.
She giggled "Yes please"
I rolled my eyes and went downstairs to make coffee.
As said in the intro, the sexual tension was building. Not sure how else to say it, but it needed to be sorted soon. Sounds stupid perhaps, but we'd had months of innuendo's, teasing, flirting, and comments. None of those things had made it easier for either of us.
But, we were strong. *Melt.* No, not a melt actually; I'm being considerate. *Wow, is that what you call it these days? Still the same thing.* Look, having been through all the shit I've been through, I can kind of see her side. And, I have no problem with it. To me, it's made our relationship stronger. Besides, I have a feeling you'll get what you've been after on this Florence trip. *You do?* Yeah, I do. *Result!*

Anyway. Enough of that. Bbq to organise today. I need to get to the butcher in Ramsey to get the meats, and some rolls from somewhere. Chrissy was doing a potato salad, and other bits. All of which needed shopping for.

And I had work to finish. Jesus. So much to do. *Fucknation, calm yourself down will you?* I am calm. *Fuck you are. Chill. You got loads of time.* I looked at my watch; it was only 07.57. *See? Chill the fuck out and go to work.* Yeah, ok, you're right. Let's get to it. I had a quick bite to eat, kissed Chrissy goodbye, and went to the office.

Ah, the office. It was great. It had turned out better than I had imagined; the décor was superb. The office was bright and airy. It didn't look or feel like an office at all, which was important to me. Yes, there were two workstations, but it was all set up so as not to look like an office. We had a seating area with leather sofas, there was a nice kitchen area, I had a guitar and amp set up so I could just walk over and play when I felt like it. Kyle had a set of electronic drums set up. He wasn't great, but learning fast. We had some great little jams, which helped us relax, and think. And then, of course, there was the gym. I say gym, it was a small room with my treadmill and an exercise bike. But, I had big windows put in to make it nice and bright. And cooler in the summer, thankfully.

All in all, I was in seventh heaven when I was there. Kyle wasn't always in office, as he had college stuff to do. Fortunately, he was in his final year, and his mock exams had gone well. He was good. Very good. I'd say better than me, but that wouldn't be saying much as I wasn't brilliant. This guy was next level. Thanks to him, we'd been able to take on more clients, and thus make more money. Chrissy had suggested offering him a partnership upon his graduation.

I wasn't sure what his future plans were, but I would love to keep him.

I'd have to sit down and chat with him about it sometime soon, before he got a job somewhere and left me in the lurch. He had already mentioned that he wanted to stay in the local area, which was promising. I think a partnership would possible seal it for him. But, that would have to wait.

I made myself a coffee, and checked my email. Nothing but positivity from our completed work. Legendary. I say the place was bliss, the only thing missing was music. I wanted a nice hifi system, Kyle wanted something more modern and Bluetooth enabled. Ongoing battle that I would eventually win. I wasn't a great fan of streaming music; the quality wasn't as good.
Plus, there's just something cool about physical media. You lose all that magic with 1's and 0's. *But a CD has digital....* Shush! It's tangible. You have to put a CD in the player. *You sad old fucker.* Whatever, I'll put in whatever I bloody well want thanks. So, erm, work. Yeah, let's have a look and see what we got. *You got nothing. You finished yesterday remember? You told Kyle to take the day off. Jesus man, where's your head at?*
Fuck. You're right. I literally had nothing to do, it was all done yesterday. I flashed p the laptop anyway and checked my email. Ha! Justice! See? Email from client requesting a change. Winner. *What the fuck ever...*
I got to work. It was only a minor change, and it only took half an hour in the end. I sent it off, and shut down. Ok. Pfffff. Now what?
Cafe?
Nah, too early. It'll be rammed.
Erm. Erm. Run?
Hmmm, I've just had coffee. Not a great idea.
Guitar?
Too early.
Fuck sake, think of something yourself then.
Well, I do have a bbq to put on later today…

Yes?

Don't know where I was going with that.

"With what?" came a voice from behind me. I knew that voice.

"Oh, you know, just talking to myself"

"I guessed as much" she said, looking around "Seen as there's no-one else here"

"To what do I owe the pleasure?" I asked. Wow, she looked lovely. Flower dress, hair in bunches, just lovely.

She did me a twirl "Glad you like"

"But I..."

"I can read minds also" she winked.

"Ah, best be careful then, as I'll deffo get in to trouble if that's true"

"Hmmm. What you doing here?"

"What?"

"I thought you said you were done for the week?"

"Yeah, I forgot. Good thing I did come in though, there was a change request"

"Ah, I see. Good thing you did then. You done now?"

"Yes, why?"

"You can take me into the city, I need to collect something from the cop shop"

"Ooh, sounds secretive, I'm in"

"Boring really, just a bunch of files"

"Still, exciting. My very own international woman of mystery"

"Dick. Come on, I've got to be there at half nine"

I shut down, locked up, and we went back to the house to get the car. The drive into PB was pretty shit; rush hour. My least favourite time of day, it was rammed with traffic. "Wow, I'm glad we don't have to commute for work" I said.

"Yeah, me too, this is pretty depressing"

"Which police station we going to?"

"Main one, I'm meeting my contact outside, so should be pretty quick"

"Gets more mysterious by the second" I winked.
"Jack, it's accounting, there's nothing mysterious about it"
"Damn it woman, let me have my fantasy"
"You're an idiot" she laughed.
We got to the police station just after half past. Her "contact" was waiting on the front steps. Looked nothing like a spy. I was disappointed. Just an office worker, standard office attire, glasses. Nothing mysterious about that. The dream crashed.
"Back in a sec" she said, and jumped out of the car. She ran over and had a brief chat with the lady. They seemed pretty friendly. But, who wouldn't be with Chrissy? She's pretty magnetic as a person.
Eventually, she took a stack of files and walked back to the car. I jumped out, and opened the boot for her.
"Turn around and wave" she said.
"What?"
"Wave to Katy"
I turned, smiled and waved. She smiled, waved back, gave Chrissy two thumbs up, and went back inside.
"Erm, what just happened? Did I just get some sort of approval?"
She laughed "Yep. I've known Katy for years, she was dying to see you"
"Well, glad I fit whatever ideal she had in mind" I said
"It's a girl thing, she just wanted to see who had stolen my heart. Her words"
"Well, thanks. And, you aint getting it back, it's mine now."
"You can keep it" she kissed me.
I closed the boot, and we drove back home.
Getting home was no drama whatsoever, traffic going out of the city was basically zero.
The sun was shining, and we had the windows down. She had selected the music today, a Sheryl Crow album. It was very upbeat and fitted right in with the summer weather.

I was about to turn into our drive when she said "No, keep driving. Let's enjoy it while it lasts"
"Yeah, why not." I got back onto the road, and we drove around for a while.
"Fancy a walk up at the nature reserve?" she asked.
"As long as we don't get wet again" I joked.
"Hey, that was your own fault"
"What? You pushed me in!"
We laughed. I drove us up there, parked, and we went for a great walk around. The place was stunning, trees in full bloom, flowers everywhere. We saw deer, a couple of otters by the lake, some herons, and of course some ducks. It was a lovely walk. Dude, you sound like an old man. Nope, just someone enjoying life. And I was enjoying life.

Tangent required.

Fainting. So, there had been only a few instances over the last month or so. They were getting less, as the stresses of the divorce and Helen's bullshit was getting more and more bearable. I could tolerate an awful lot more these days. Crying still happened, but only because I missed the kids. They were down in Huntingdon, and our weekend together had become shorter because of it.
I drove them home, of course. But they usually got the bus from there to mine on Fridays. I say bus; three different buses. It was shit for them, but they didn't complain. I'm sure Elsie didn't really mind the bus journey so much. It was like a little adventure for her. James on the other hand hated it. His anger towards his mother was increasing. We'd had a few chats about it, and I was helping him cope. I think he just needs an outlet to vent his frustrations. I was happy to be the enabler.

"You ok there?"
"What? Oh, yeah, just lost in thought"
"James?"
"Yeah. He worries me."
"He's pretty angry"
"Yes, I know"
"He has every right to be"
"I know that too. But he needs to learn to deal with it or it'll affect his life"
"So…….?"
"So?"
"So, what you going to do?"
"I'm already talking to him, letting him vent down"
"But it's not helping"
"No, it's not" I hated admitting it, but it really wasn't.
"How about counselling?"
"He's not me" I said automatically.
"Hey, whoa, steady on. I wasn't suggesting that. I was thinking maybe someone he can talk to without any fears of judgement"
"I don't judge him" I said defensively.
"You're his dad Jack. Think about it"
"Yeah, ok, you have a point"
"I know someone"
"You do?"
"Yes. Katy? The woman we saw earlier? She's a police counsellor"
"He needs police counseling?"
"No you dick, she specialises in trauma care"
"Ah, like post shooting?
"That doesn't happen here, but yeah, that kind of thing"
"You think it would help? You think she would want to?"
"Yes, and yes. You want me to set up a meeting?"
Well, James has school, so…"

"No, just with you to start, so you can talk about what you're worried about and give her some background info"
"Ah, I see. Yeah, sure"
"Cool, I'll set it up"

And she did; I was meeting with Katy next Monday afternoon. (Not tomorrow!)

"We should get back" she said, tapping her watch.
"Shit, of course. You have work to do?"
"Nope, but you do"
"I do?" I do? *Yes, you do.*
"Bbq?" quizzical.
"Ah, yeah, right. Bbq. I need to go to the butcher in Ramsey and then to Tesco over in Chatteris?"
"Sounds like a plan. Did you get the table and chairs from your parents?"
"Yep, it's all in the bar"
"Excellent. Just shopping and prep work to do then"
"Indeed"
"I'll change the kid's beds in case we have stay overs"
"Good idea" I said, and kissed her. "I love you"
"I love you too"
We got back to the car, and drove off to Ramsey.

The butcher in Ramsey was a friend of my dad, so I got a decent discount.
"Morning Jack, all ready for you"
"Morning Bill, you good?" I asked.
"I am thanks" he smiled "I got everything you need, was there anything else you needed?"
"Nope, this should do nicely" I said, looking at the bags. There was loads; various types of sausage, same with burgers, some belly pork, and chicken kebabs.

"Excellent. All paid and good to go" Bill said.
"It is?" I said, wallet in hand.
"Yep, your dad squared up when he was here this morning" he winked.
"Hmmm. Ok. I'll chat to him later"
He just laughed, and handed me the bags "Have a great party"

"Wow, that was nice of your dad" Chrissy said as we walked back to the car.
"Yes, wasn't it just" I had never been comfortable with people paying for stuff for me.

Tangent, so I don't have to go into it in the story?

People paying for stuff for me. Never been a fan. I make enough money to pay my own way. I know I probably shouldn't think that way, and just be graceful, but; it just niggled at me. I know what you're thinking: *But Chrissy is paying for soooo much, how come you're not distraught about that?*
Well, I am. But, it is a little different. We're in a growing relationship, and I don't want to rock the boat. Also, that isn't going to be something that would happen much more after this. In the years to come, I would more than make up for it, believe me.
I know my dad was being kind, and I wasn't really going to talk to him about it. I would accept graciously, and get him a few beers. That's how I'd always handled these things. Not always with beer mind...

"Yes, it really was, so you don't have to argue it. Just thank him, ok?"
"What?"
"Mind reader, told you" she winked.
Holy fuck. My thoughts exactly...

"I will. You though. You scare me. Witchcraft"
"You calling me a witch?" she said, with shoulder punch accompaniment.
"Ouch. Yes, I was actually" I said, rubbing my shoulder "A fit witch though"
"Ah, that's ok then" she smiled "You want to take this stuff back first? Get it in the fridge?"
"Yeah, sure"
We drove home, packed the meat into the already full fridge, and then went on to the Tesco in Chatteris.
As we drove into the village, Chrissy asked "Hey, when's your next appointment?"
"Oh, erm, next Thursday" I hadn't actually thought about it at all, I was super happy at the moment. I had a bar, a gorgeous partner, awesome kids, and a fucking ex-wife. Hmmmm. *Not sure that last one is a positive mate.* Yeah, I think you're right there. Although she had been fairly silent recently. I hadn't had any messages from her for a while. I guess she was happily shacked up with whatever his name. *What is his name?* Who gives a fuck? *Truth.* Anyway, don't want to be thinking about her.
"You ok there?" Chrissy asked
"Eh? Oh, yeah, just thinking about stuff, you know"
"Oh, yeah, I know. As long as it's not about her" she warned.
"No. Ok, maybe. I was only thinking that I hadn't heard anything from her for a while"
"Ugh. Surely that's only a good thing?"
"Yes, that's what I thought. Sorry"
"It's ok, I know she has to be in your life in some small way. I just don't like it I guess"
"I get it, it's not great for me either you know. I'd rather she was just gone forever"
"Yeah, I know. Sorry. Anyways, we here"
"So we are" I parked up, and we went in.

The air-conditioning was not particularly pleasant, cold and dry. I suppose most liked it, a bit of an escape from the warmth outside. Weird isn't it? We spend all year wishing for summer, then welcome air conditioning.
"Yeah, weird isn't it. I'm not really a fan of it either to be honest" Chrissy said.
Fuck me lad, get that gob of yours under control. Damn. What the hell was I doing?
"People eh?" I said, trying to deflect from the fact that I was going mad.
"Speaking your thoughts out loud is getting to be a bit of a habit" Chrissy commented.
I hung my head "Yeah, I know. I'll speak to Pam about it next week. It's getting on my nerves, and could land me in the shit properly one day"
"Yes, it probably will" she laughed "Though you're safe with me" she ruffled my hair.
"Thanks. I really need to work on it"
We browsed around for a bit, throwing the odd bits and pieces for the bbq into the trolley.
"Morning Jack"
Holy fucking shit. I knew that voice. Helen's dad, Phil.
I turned, and there he was right behind us.
"Oh, Mr Stevens, how are you?" I managed from beneath my cloak of embarrassment.
"Mr Stevens? Look Jack, I know you probably don't feel comfortable, but you can still call me Phil you know?" He held out his hand.
I took his hand and shook it. "Yeah, sorry. Hi Phil, how are you?"
"I'm ok, you know. Could be better eh"
"Yeah, I know"
"This is?" he said, looking at Chrissy.
"Chrissy" she said, holding out her hand.

"Nice to meet you Chrissy" he said, shaking her hand with a smile.
"Well, I won't hold you up, I know it's probably pretty awkward for you. Take care of yourself Jack" he said, putting his hand on my shoulder.
"Thanks Phil, you too"
He held his hand on my shoulder for another second or so, with a look of, I don't know? Regret? Sympathy?
"Nice to meet you Chrissy" he said with a smile "Take care of him will you?"
"I will Mr Stevens" she said.
"Please, it's Phil. My dad was Mr Stevens" he said.
"Phil" she said.
"Have a great day" he smiled, turned away, and walked off towards the bakery section.
I stood watching him go; he turned and gave me a wave, then disappeared around a corner.
I would never see him again; he would be dead in two weeks.
I'm glad I got that opportunity for reconciliation before he died.

"Wow" Chrissy said "That was a bit weird. But, he seems nice"
"He's a nice guy." I said. "We were very close"
"He seemed very friendly towards you though" she said, confused.
"I wrote him a letter after the divorce, giving him my side of events. I didn't want him thinking I'd cheated on his daughter"
"I can understand that. He must have been relived to read it"
"I don't know, I never got a response, but I'm glad I got my side across"
"He believed you" she said.
"How do you know?"
"Did you not see the look in his eye? The way he held his hand on your shoulder? He cares about you a lot, and misses you. It's obvious he doesn't blame you"

"Really?"
"Yeah, trust me. It was written all over him"
That made me happy. "I'm glad. He's such a nice man"
"I bet he is"
She put her arms around me and hugged me tight. "Don't fall apart here ok? Hold it together" she whispered in my ear.
I nodded my head. She knew; I was teetering on the edge. *Deep breaths Jack, come on.*
I took a few deep ones, and got it together. "Ok, I'm good" *No you're not.* Ok, I'm not, but I'll manage.
"That's good enough" she winked "Come on" *Fuck sake!*
We carried on around the shop, just filling the trolley with stuff. Mostly beer, to make me happy. I liked having a wide variety of ales in the bar.
"You have enough beer in there?" Chrissy joked.
"You think we need more?" I asked seriously.
"Are you kidding?"
"Yeah" I nudged her. "Let's get out of here before I bankrupt myself"
We checked out, and drove home, bottles rattling in the boot.

Time check. Ok, it's 12.14.
Lunch?
What? I need to make sure the garden is tidy, and prepare salads and stuff.
Mate, you have ages. What's your fucking beef?
Fair enough, you're right.
Of course I am. Take her for lunch at Steve's.
Plan. Like it.
Good. Chill the fuck out. There's hardly anything to do here. Relax.
Ok, I get the fucking picture.
"Hey, you fancy lunch?"
"Yeah, I could eat"
"Wanna go over to Steve's?"

"You mind if we eat here?" Eh?
"You sure?"
"Yeah, I just want to sit in the garden and relax in silence, it's going to be busy enough later"
"Good point" I conceded.
"You don't mind?"
I kissed her. "Of course not. You sit, I'll get some food"
She leaned back on the garden chair, and soaked up a bit of sun. I went off and fixed us a nice ham salad wrap each, with a jug of juice. We ate mostly in silence, which was ok with me. She was right; it was going to be manic enough later on. I say manic, there weren't that many people coming. Me, Chrissy, Steve and Willow, Mum and Dad, Kyle and his partner, Katy and her husband, and architect friend Astrid. I'm sure Steve would play the amazing host, making it a great night. He was so much better at that stuff that I was, he knew this of course, but he also knew I didn't mind. Someone had to be the party animal; it certainly wasn't me. Although… We'd done some pretty fucked up stuff in the past… *Yeah you did! Proud moments!* Sure, but let's just leave it in the past shall we. *Ugh, you're such a drip.*
"How you feeling?" Chrissy asked after we had cleared away the lunch dishes.
"Me? I'm ok"
"Sure?" What? *Read between the lines dickhead…*
Ah, got it. Am I ok because I'm not seeing the kids this weekend?
"Yes"
"What? Oh. I did it again"
She just laughed. "You have to watch that"
I rolled my eyes. "Hmm. Yes, I am ok not seeing the kids."
"Sure?" she said again. *She can see right through your mask…*
"Ok, no I'm not. But, I'm keeping it together"
"Good. Come sit" she patted the chair next to hers.
I sat, and we lay back, holding hands.

"Jack"
Chrissy.
Shaking.
"What?"
"Wake up, it's just gone two"
I woke with a start "Shit. I fell asleep"
"Yes, you did" she laughed.
"Fuck. I need to make salad and stuff" I said getting up.
"Chill, it's done" Steve said.
"Eh? When did you get here?" I said, confused.
"About an hour ago. We did the lunch rush, then closed early to come help out"
I rubbed my eyes. "You didn't need to"
"I know, but I wanted to make sure the food was fucking edible didn't I?" he said with a wink.
"Knob. You want a beer?"
"Fuck aye. Come on sleepyhead" He pulled me out of my seat, and we went into the bar, where Willow was busy decorating.
"Oh look who's decided to join us!" she said, and kissed my cheek.
"You spend too much time around him" I joked.
"Hey!" Steve said.
"What?"
"Feelings?" he said pointing at himself.
We all laughed.
"You're all a bunch of dicks" he said. "Except you" he kissed Willows bump.
I got us beer from the fridge, and we toasted to good friends and a fucking awesome night ahead. Hopefully.
Yeah, let's get fucked up!
No, let's not.
Man, you're such a fucking melt, what happened to you??
I grew up?
Ugh, whatever.

There was no "getting fucked up" whilst we prepped; we had one beer. Too much to do, no time for drinking. We had everything ready by four, and people weren't coming till six, so we just sat at the table, chilling out after all the effort.
"Anyone fancy a walk along the canal?" Willow asked after a few minutes
"Yeah, why not" Steve said.
"Good idea" Chrissy agreed.
The weather was awesome; it was about 25 degrees, sunny, partly cloudy. Perfect in other words. I don't do well in heat, so it was enough for me. We went for a walk down the tow path, which was much needed. It cleared my head, and we got back feeling refreshed and ready for the party.
Frank the Tank? Fuck no. *Sigh…*

I did a final check to make sure everything was ready, then fired up the bbq. Half hour till people started turning up. I went inside and took a pill.
Good plan. Last thing we need now is a breakdown.
I'm on it.
Good lad.
Thanks. I think.
You ready for this?
For what?
All these people. It's going to be busy.
Yeah, I think so.
Ok, let's hope so eh.
Like I said, I'm on it.
"On what?" Steve asked.
"Hmm? Oh, you know, all the people coming. Going to be busy"
"You'll be fine" he said putting his arm around me "I'm here to help"
"Thanks bud"

He kissed my head, and went off to see how Willow was doing.
Chrissy tapped me on the shoulder.
I turned "Yes? Oh. Wow. Jesus" *Putting it lightly; fuck me.*
"You like?" she did a twirl, and the summer dress she had changed into flared out showing a nice amount of leg.
"Oh I like" I said.
"Good" she kissed my nose and went off into the kitchen. I stood for a moment, just taking it in. What a woman. *And she smells so good.* Yeah, she does.

Cue the doorbell.
Ring Ring…
And so it begins…
Deep breath.

My fears were obviously totally unfounded; it was a fantastic night. There was so much laughter and happiness. I was watching carefully what I was drinking, ensuring I didn't go too far. Everyone that knows me, knows that "Jack? Quiet guy. But get a few drinks down him…." I didn't mind that reputation, I just needed to ensure I didn't go too far. Chatty Jack is good. Drunk Jack is not good.

I was at my station, manning the bbq. This was my safe place; always busy, and always something to talk about if someone came over. Steve came over regularly to check on me.
"You ok brother?" "I'm good thanks mate. Could do with a fresh beer though" "On it" He'd pat my shoulder and walk off happy. Standing back, observing the scene, I found it interesting how people were different after a few drinks.
Kyle was talking far more than usual. *That's not difficult though eh, he hardly says a word!* True, hence it was noticeable that he was walking around speaking to everyone.

I finished cooking, dished up, and put the plates of meat on a table for people to help themselves to. I grabbed a burger, and made the rounds. I was in a safe zone. I felt at ease around these people. I had none of the usual fears of anxiety. It was great, brilliant in fact.

The night passed without issues of any kind. It was a complete success in fact. By around 11 o'clock, we found ourselves closing the front door on our last leaver.

Chrissy hugged me, and said "You did amazingly well, you should be proud"

"Thanks, I was worried, not going to lie. But, I feel comfortable around these people."

"Good, I could see as much. You were talking to everyone, without any drama"

"I had Steve checking on my occasionally, so was ok really"

"I saw, bless him, he really loves you"

"Yeah, like brothers"

"Exactly like brothers" she kissed me. "Let's tidy and go to bed"

We tidied and went to bed.

Chrissy fell asleep rapidly, and I thought I would to. However, I lay awake for ages; I was still on a high. This wasn't going to be a great night for sleep. I put my headphones in and went to see what Mr Holmes had in store for me tonight.

After about an hour of dashing through the streets of Victorian London, I faded out...

Yeah. That was a long chapter eh? Makes a difference from the previous 3 books. Usually the first chapter is fairly short. I have the feeling this is going to be a sizeable book...

Day 2, Monday, 11th of June.

Hey.
Eh?
Yo!
What??
Wake up!
Fuck off, I'm tired.
Seriously. Wake up.
Why?
I'll give you a choice; wake up now, or piss the bed.
Ah.
Got it now?
Yeah, fair point.
I got up. My bladder was screaming.
Still half asleep, I made my way to the loo. Better.
I stumbled my way back to be in the half light of morning.
Chrissy was gone.
What? A quick look at the clock told me why; it was 08.00. She was up for work.
Sounds like a good idea, maybe you should do the same?
Yeah, probably. I turned around and headed for the shower.
A quick shower in lukewarm water woke me up. I brushed my teeth, and got dressed.
Downstairs, Chrissy was sat at the kitchen table drinking coffee. The sunlight was catching her hair, making it glow. She looked beautiful.
"Thank you, I do try" she winked.
The fuck?
Dude! Control your fucking mind already!
Not sure how.
Work it out.

"You want coffee?" she asked, getting up.
"Yeah, if there is any" I sat down.
She came over with a cup of hot coffee "Here, you look like you need it"
"I'm not hungover" I said "I feel fine. Just tired"
"Well, that's good, and bad I suppose. Why so tired?"
"I find social occasions exhausting" I said "They drain me"
"How so?" she asked, sipping her coffee.
"I think keeping up a brave face or pretending to be someone I'm not takes an awful lot of energy. Does that make sense?"
"Think so, like a mental exhaustion?"
"Yeah, exactly"
"I get that too sometimes, after a hard day at work. Not necessarily physically hard, but mentally hard"
"Its hard work keeping up appearances" I said "It's like wearing a mask all evening"
"I think I understand, must be hard for you"
"Yeah, it is. Even if I feel totally at ease with people, it's still difficult"

Tangent?

So, this is an actual thing, not something I came up with. Check it on the interweb. Wearing a mask, pretending to be someone you aren't. If you're social anxious, you have to wear a mask in social situations to pretend you're "normal". It's exhausting keeping up the act, especially if the social goes on for a long time. I have experience with it, and I know others that do also. It's tiring. I always thought there was something wrong with me physically causing constant tiredness, but it's a mental thing. Look it up. If you're a mask wearer; I empathise. Back to it.

She ruffled my hair, and said "Why don't you take a day off?"

"I have too much work to do this week" Do you? Dunno, just guessing.
"Well, why don't you go in and check out what's on this week and make a call"
"Yeah, I will"
"You could do with a rest, you worked really late all last week"
She was right, Kyle and I had burned a lot of hours to get all of our work done so we could enjoy the weekend.
"Ok, I'll go in and see what there is"
"Good" she said, and stood "I'm off to the office, got a meeting in five" She leaned down and kissed me "See you later, take it easy today, ok?"
"Ok, I will. Love you"
"Love you too".
She went off upstairs holding a mug, and a piece of toast in her mouth. I finished my coffee, and went off to the office. It was lovely outside, starting to get warm already. It was quite busy out, as busy as Ramsey Forty Foot gets I suppose, so it's relative…
The short walk to the office was great; it was always good to be out in the fresh air. Kyle was already in when I got there.
"Morning" he said cheerfully when I walked in. How I admired the young; they could party and be fresh as a daisy the following day.
"Morning, we got much on this week?"
"Erm, let's see…Enough to keep us busy till Thursday I think"
"That's music to my ears" I said, plonking down at my desk.
"You ok?" he asked.
"Yeah, just tired. Very tired."
"You should go home and get some sleep, I can manage here till later if you want" he offered.
"I think I'll stay and just finish at lunch time if that's ok?" I asked.
"You're the boss" he said.

"Hmmmm. About that" I started.

"Hmm?"

"I've been thinking about the future"

"Uh-oh, should I be worried?"

"Not at all. I've just been thinking about the business."

"Ok…"

"Let me ask you something. What are your plans for the future? I mean, you finish your course soon. What comes after?"

"Wow, erm, I hadn't really thought about it to be fair"

"You're a bright lad Kyle, you could do well somewhere and make a lot of money"

"That would mean moving away from here though" he said.

"Yes, I guess it would."

"Are you expecting me to leave?" he asked.

"I don't know. I guess I sort of am. Like I said, you're incredibly good, you could get a job anywhere"

"Would you want me to leave?" he asked.

"Not at all"

"Hmm. Well, I hadn't planned on leaving, if that puts your mind at ease. If I get a job somewhere else, I'd have to move away from Jasper. He has a great job, with a promising career where he is. It would be unfair to expect him to move"

"You're saying all the right things" I said.

"I am?" he looked confused.

"I have a proposition"

"Ok…"

"I want you to be an equal share partner in the business" I said.

"Wow" he was taken aback. "You sure?"

"Kyle, I couldn't run this business alone, you know that. We are ever expanding, and will probably have to take on someone else soon too"

"True, things are looking good" he said.

"Very good, this sector is booming."

"So what would that mean?"

"You'd own 50% of the business, with an income to match that. Not promising your income will sky rocket, but as we get more work in, it will go up in-line with that"

"Part owner? You sure?"

"Of the business, yes, absolutely. You don't want to?"

"I'm not sure I deserve it, but yes, I would very much like to. How much would I need to invest?"

"Invest?"

"Yes, I'd need to invest in order to make it fair surely?"

"Ah, you mean this place?" I said, indicating the office. "Chrissy owns the building, we pay rent. No investment needed"

"Ok"

"You need time to think, I understand"

"No, no. No I don't. I accept. If that's ok?"

I shook his hand "Of course it is. Welcome aboard partner" I smiled.

He beamed "Thanks boss"

"Not boss, partner" I said.

"Thanks partner"

"Better. Hopefully it gives you a better feeling about your future and career" I said.

"It gives me exactly what I wanted" he said happily "I didn't want to move, and was happy to stay here. You know, before"

"Understood. That makes me happy. I'll get the solicitor to draw up the necessary paperwork and let you know when it's ready for signature"

"I'm so happy right now" he said, with obvious enthusiasm

"You want to celebrate with breakfast at the cafe?" he asked

"My treat"

"Sure. Let's go… partner"

"That'll take some getting used to" he said.

I laughed, patted him on the back, and we left for the cafe. It felt good to make someone happy.

It felt good to make me happy too.

It was a big relief to have him accept, I was worried he'd be out as soon as he finished his course. He was a level headed, old fashioned type of lad though; he didn't want to upset his partner, even at the cost of his own career. I wasn't quite sure what his partner did, but I'm sure he will appreciate the news when Kyle tells him.

Things were looking bright.

Tinkle.

"Well fuck me sideways, look who's here"
Kyle laughed "Morning Mr Fletcher"
"Wow, really? My dad is Mr Fletcher. Call me Steve for fuck sake"
"Morning Steve"
"Better!" he smiled "Now then, what can I do for you gentlemen?"
"Breakfast" I said.
"Coming up. Go sit"
We sat at my usual table, though could have sat anywhere, the breakfast rush was over and it was fairly quiet. No sign of Willow.
"Hey, you need a hand?" I shouted.
"Help yourself to coffee" he shouted back "Willow is out at the wholesaler"
"Roger that" I got up and walked over to the machine. "What you fancy?" I asked Kyle
"Cappuccino?" he asked.
"No problem" I went to work. I loved working this machine. Although Steve had purchased all new machines for the cafe, it was just a newer model of the old one, and I could still work it. I made myself a latte first, then did Kyle's cap.
"Here you go" I said, putting the cup down in front of him.

"Wow, you're a barista too?" he asked "Anything you don't do?"
"Well, I used to help Steve out a lot, so he put me on a course"
"Good skill to have" he said, and took a sip "Wow, nice"
"Thank you"
"You mind if I tell Jasper tonight?"
"About the partnership?"
"Yeah, I know the paperwork is still to be done, but is it ok to tell him now?"
"Of course, I'm sure he'll be over the moon"
"He will be"
"Good, it's all worked out for the best"
"It has. Thank you Jack. I mean it. You have no idea how happy I am"
"I have a good imagination, and I'm happy it was what you wanted. I was never sure"
"Well, it was, is. Thank you"
"You're welcome. I couldn't imagine a better partner"
"Cheers to that" he said.
"Cheers to what?" Steve said, walking out with two plates of hot breakfast.
"Steve, meet my new business partner Kyle" I said.
"Fucking hell lad, well done" he put the plates down and shook his hand.
"Thank you Steve, it's made my day. My week, probably my life"
"You say that now. You have to deal with this fucknut now" he said, nodding towards me
"Ahem, fucknuts have ears…"
"You just treat this kid right, ok?"
"Of course, 50-50 share. Paperwork is being drawn up"
"Good. Well done Kyle, I'm sure he recognises how lucky he is that you accepted"
"I'm sure he is" he laughed.

"Wow. Right here guys. Right here" I said
We had a good laugh, then tucked into our food.
"Wow, needed that" Kyle said, leaning back with satisfaction.
"Yep, me too" I added
"Everything ok over there?" Steve said form the counter.
"Yes sir, all good thank you"
"Glad to hear it"
"Right, you want to head back and get some work done?" I asked.
"Yep, let me just square up" he stood and started walking over to Steve.
"No need" he said "All taken care of"
"Eh? You sure?" he asked.
"Yeah, don't worry about it"
"Ok, well, thank you"
"Don't thank me" he said "Thank him" he nodded in my direction.
Kyle turned "You paid?"
"Technically, no, but I guess"
"Confusion"
Steve spoke up from behind him "This penis never pays for anything, yet mysteriously, there's always money in the tip jar to cover it" he said "He thinks I don't know"
"He did…" I said
"But I've always known" Steve said.
"Busted" Kyle said, looking at me.
I held my hands up "Guilty"
"As fuck" Steve added.
"Sorry" I said.
"You don't need to do that" Stave said "You know that right?"
"I do, but it makes me feel better" (Refer to my tangent about people paying for stuff)
"I know" he said, conceding "You do whatever you need to do matey"

"Oh, I will" I said.

"Fuck you"

"Fuck you very much too" I said.

"Everything ok here?" Kyle asked, unsure.

"Of course" Steve said. He came out and gave me a bear hug "Always. You guys have a great day"

"Thanks" I said.

"Now get the fuck out"

We laughed, and walked back to the office.

"You guys obviously have history" Kyle said as we walked.

Yes. Yes we do" I said "Good history"

"He seems like the best kind of friend anyone could have. I'm envious"

"He is that. He's like a brother to me"

"You're lucky" he said.

"I'm sure we all have friends like that though"

"Not really" he said.

"Oh, surely you have plenty of friends" I asked.

"No, not like that for sure. Being gay kind of puts people off, you know?"

"Sorry. That must be hard"

"Yeah, it's not an easy journey. But, I have Jasper"

"You have all of us here too" I said, putting my arm around his shoulders "Don't forget that"

"That's good to know" he said "I appreciate that"

"We're all a big family, and you're part of that too" I reassured him.

"I like the idea of that"

We walked the rest of the way in silence. I was sure there was more behind his last statement, but thought it was perhaps the wrong time to ask about it.

"Right, what we got on this week?" I asked as we sat at our desks.

"I'll send you over the files for the week, let me know what you want me to do" Kyle responded.
"We're partners now, why don't you decide which ones you want to do, and give me the rest?"
"You sure?"
"Yeah, works for me. I'd rather you worked on what you wanted rather than whatever I give you"
Few minutes later, I received the files, and we both went to work.

"You want a drink?"
"What?" I said, looking up.
"You want a drink?" Kyle was stood at the fridge.
"Oh, yeah, please. What time is it?"
"It's almost half past twelve" he said.
"Wow, already?"
"Yep. Time flies eh" he threw over a bottle of orange juice.
I caught it, and drank greedily. "I've just finished a vid. You mind if I disappear in a minute?" I said
"Me?"
"Partners remember?"
"Ah. No, I don't mind at all. I can finish one more this afternoon, and leave by two if that's ok?"
"Leave whenever you feel" I said with a wink. "I'm sure we're responsible enough to manage our time"
"Cool, thanks"
"Right, you have the bridge Captain" I said, knowing he was a big Trekkie.
"Thank you Captain" he nodded with a smile.
I grabbed my phone and headed home. I needed sleep. *Yawn, yeah you do.*
When I got home, I heard Chrissy talking away upstairs, she was in a meeting.

I popped my head in and waved to let her know I was home, and made a gesture indicating I was going for a snooze. She winked, and blew me a kiss.

I fell down on to the bed, and blacked out completely. It was pure bliss; vivid dreams and much needed downtime. I was dreaming about Chrissy riding a horse on a rainbow (told you, weird), when the world starting shaking. Realising it wasn't in my dream, but real, I woke. *Fuck sake, she was about to take her kit off!*
"Wha?"
"Wha? Lol. Hello. Thought you'd like to know it's almost five" Chrissy said.
"It's what?" I said, sitting up with shock.
"It's almost five"
"Shit. Really. Dammit"
"Hey, don't worry about it, its ok"
"No, I missed my appointment"
"Oh, well, I'm sure you can rearrange right?"
"Yeah, sure. You're right. I'll call her now"
"Let me do that, you go shower"
"Sure?"
"Yeah, go on, I'll call her now and ask her to send you an appointment"
"Ok, thank you" I got up and went for a shower to wake up.
"Oh, and Jack?" she asked as I was walking away.
"Yes?" I turned.
"You're cute when you sleep" she winked.
"Thanks" I chuckled, and trundled into the bathroom.

I stood in the shower for ages, it felt great and I didn't want to get out. There was a knock at the door, and Chrissy came in
"Jack, you ok?" She asked.
"Yeah, sorry. Just enjoying the moment"

She looked me up and down, smiled, and walked out "Ok, dinner will be ready soon"
Dude, she just totally checked us out. Didn't she just.
I finished up and got out. Looking at myself in the mirror, I thought I looked tired. *Yeah, you do.* Thanks for that. I needed exercise. Tomorrow morning I'd go for a run before work.
I dressed and went down to see what was for dinner. "Smells good" I said, walking in
"Mmmm, have a seat, almost ready" she said.
I sat down, and she put a glass of wine in front of me. "Two minutes"
"Ok" I took a sip of the wine and watched her. She was a natural in the kitchen. She served up, and it looked as good as it smelled. "Wow, this looks good. What we got?"
"Crab ravioli in a dill sauce" she beamed with pride.
"Wow, all fresh made?"
"Yep, I saw it on the telly and thought I'd give it a go"
"Well, it sure is nice" I said, with a mouth full of food.
She giggled "Thanks"

Dinner was superb, and we lay on the sofa for ages after, just enjoying eachother's company. It was too early to go to bed, so I channel surfed for a bit to kill time. Eventually, we settled on an episode of Silent Witness. Not my favourite, but Chrissy seemed to like it. So much so that she fell asleep after ten minutes. I watched till the end, then woke her up.
"Come on, let's get you to bed"
She yawned and followed me up.
By the time I'd brushed my teeth, she was sparked.
I had a feeling I wouldn't be far behind her.
Not sure headphones were rquired…..

Day 3, Tuesday, 12th of June.

True to my word, I went for a run before work. I really needed it, and was glad I dragged myself out. It was early, and still a bit cold. As I ran along, the fog in my mind was lifting slowly like the thin mist that hung over the canal, and I ended my run in a super good mood. I sat on the bridge for a bit afterwards, stretching and just enjoying the world around me. Things were good. No, things were great. I couldn't believe where my life was at, everything was positive.
It is?
What?
Erm, nothing.
No, wait. What do you mean? Oh. Shit. The kids. I hadn't seen them for two weeks. I hadn't even thought about them all weekend. What kind of father doesn't even think about his children? *No, no, stop it now!* Too late. An instant feeling of despair and utter guilt fell over me like a cold fog. The world faded out; the sounds of nature around me slowly dimmed away to silence, the bright sunlight slowly extinguishing to darkness. I was out.
"Jack!" Wow, loud, no need. "Jack? Wake up!" What? I'm not asleep…
If I'm not sleeping, why is it dark? I told my brain to open my eyes, and it slowly but surely started responding. Light seeped in, and the world came back into focus. I'm lying down.
"Jack? Jesus, what the fuck?"
"Who..?"
"It's me, Willow. Hey, you ok? What happened?"
"Willow" realisation came like a flash "Shit. I fainted"
"Fuck. You need an ambulance?" she sounded panicky.

"No, no, it's ok. I'll be fine" I tried sitting up, but struggled. Willow helped me to get sat up against the bridge.
"Fuck Jack, fuck" she said, both concerned and confused.
"Hey. I'm ok, really. It happens sometimes."
"What? Since when?"
"Oh, it's been happening for a while"
"What?" she said incredulously and punched my shoulder "And you didn't think to tell anyone?"
"Ouch!" I replied, rubbing my shoulder. "I thought I had?"
She rolled her eyes "You told Steve"
"Of course"
"I'll have words, he should have told me. No, *you* should have told me" she punched my shoulder again.
"Aargh! Fuck!"
"You deserve it, and he'll get the same. You idiot" If I was hurt physically, she was obviously hurt emotionally.
"I'm really sorry. I thought Steve would have told you"
"I would have thought so too" she said. "Ok, get up, let's get you home"
"I can walk, I'll be fine" I protested
"Don't be an even bigger dick than you are already. I'll walk you home"
Don't protest. I won't. "You're right"
I felt like an idiot, and I had upset Willow. But worse was to come…
"What the fucking hell?"
"You're angry"
"No fucking shit. That's it. You're not allowed out on your own" she said sternly.
"What?"
"Don't even think of arguing" she warned, holding up an accusing finger.
Dude, just agree…
"Ok" I said meekly.

"What was that?" she said angrily, raising her eyebrows. She looked super cute.

"Ok!" I said smiling "I won't"

"Good. Go have a shower" she ordered, pointing up the stairs. I did as I was told whilst she talked to Willow in the kitchen. I couldn't hear what they were saying about me, but I'm sure it wasn't complimentary.

Fuck sake! I was so angry with myself. This was getting out of control. I needed to see Pam, asap. Thursday seemed to far away. *You sure she can help?* What? *This not a medical matter?* No, we've been through that already. I need to get my head better. The realisation I had on the bridge was immediate and unexpected. I need to ensure I deal with stuff like this better. If I don't see the kids, I need to talk about it instead of keeping it inside. I would have a chat with Chrissy when she'd calmed down a bit, her help was essential here.

I got out of my running kit and had a shower. I must have been in there for a while, because there was a knock on the door "You ok in there?"

"It's unlocked" I shouted.

She came in and stood leaning against the sink. "How you feeling?"

Her voice was different now, the anger gone. She was concerned, considerate, caring.

"I'm ok, really" I said.

"Good" she said "I'm sorry for shouting. I'm just worried"

"It's ok, I deserved it, but have a way to possibly prevent it happening again"

You do?" she asked.

"I do, but would prefer talking when I'm dressed if that's ok"

She looked embarrassed "Oh, yes, of course. Sorry, I'll erm, I'll see you downstairs" she retreated hurriedly and closed the door.

Dude! She... Not a good time, fuck off. *Ok...*

39

I stood under the hot shower for a minute or so longer, then got out and dried off.
Wow. What a morning. And it was only 8 o'clock. I text Kyle to tell him I'd be a bit late in, and went downstairs.
Chrissy was sat at the kitchen table, and there were two how mugs of coffee on the table.
I sat down, took a deep breath, and told her my idea. She took a moment to think, then replied.
"So, I think it's a good idea, and I am more than willing to help. I will make a point of asking how you are if the kids don't come. But..."
"Yes?"
"I would like you to get seen by the doctor again. Just to be safe, you know? Maybe he can refer you for a scan?"
"Wow, a scan?" I hadn't even thought of that. What if there was something wrong? Jesus.
"Please? It would put both our minds at ease I think?"
She was right of course...
"Ok, I'll make an appointment"
She took my hands "Thank you"
"It's a good idea. As much as the thought of it scares me."
"I'll go with you if you get the referral"
"Thanks"
"I'm just worried about you fainting somewhere, or even whilst driving. You know?"
"Yeah, I get it. You can be my personal chauffeur from now on then" I winked.
"Happy to oblige sir" She looked at her watch. "Shit, I have a meeting" she jumped up, kissed me and ran upstairs "See you later, let me know if you need me" she called whilst running up the stairs.
It was almost nine o'clock, Kyle was probable elbow deep in work already. Feeling guilty, I finished my coffee and made my way to the office.

40

"Hey Kyle, Sorry I'm so late" I said walking in.
"Morning Jack" he said, looking up from his computer "You ok?"
"Yeah, all good, thanks for asking. How we doing this week?"
"Twenty two vids, 16 big, rest small"
Concise. "Wow, that's not too bad" I did the mental math; it would make a profit.
"Hey Jack..." Kyle started.
"Yeah?"
"So I had a chat with Jas, about the partnership?"
"Yes…"
"He's over the moon" he beamed "You have no idea how happy you have made us, it's such a relief that I don't have to move away"
"Hey, that's amazing news, I'm glad it made you both happy"
"I hope you don't mind, but we got you something to say thank you"
"Ach, you didn't need to" I said.
"We wanted to. Like I said, you have no idea what you have done for me. For us. So, we got you this" He handed me an envelope "It's not much, but we thought you'd like it"
I took the envelope and opened it. Inside were two tickets to see the Killers at the Cresset in PB next month.
"Wow!"
"You like?" he asked, uncertain.
"I love" I said, and hugged him "Thank you"
He wasn't used to being hugged, so it was a bit awkward, but it needed to be done.
"You really didn't need to" I said after letting him go.
He composed himself "Well, you know, I kind of thought it would be nice"
"It was very nice. Not necessary, but totally appreciated. Thank you"

"You're welcome. Partner" The last word still sounded hesitant.
"I see a bright future for us, partner" I winked.
He smiled. He would eventually relax more, and accept his new position, but right now, it was still a novelty.
"Show me what you got for me" I said, smiling.
We went through the work for the week, divided it up, and got on with it.

"Hey Jack"
"Hmmmm?" I said, absent mindedly.
"It's almost one o'clock"
"What?" I looked at the clock "Oh, shit"
"You maybe want to do lunch?" he said, with his usual coyness.
"Sure thing" I saved my work, and got up "What you thinking?"
"Oh, erm..." He looked like a deer caught in the headlights. I was joking of course; options were limited to... Steve's café.
I laughed and patted him on the shoulder "Come on partner"

The tinkle of the doorbell was not accompanied by the usual barrage of abuse. Ok, weird...
Steve was stood behind the counter, helping a lady with her order. He looked up and said "Alright mate, with you in a sec"
Alright mate? Wtf? I looked at Kyle, and he looked as confused as I was. He shrugged his shoulders.
"Thanks Doris, you have a great day" he said as the lady went off to a table.
"Right, gents, how can I help?" he asked.
"Gents?" I asked "You ok?"
"Me? Yep, right as rain"
"Get the fuck out. What's going on?" I insisted.
"Alright, alright, keep it down. Been told off haven't I?" he said, nodding towards Willow.
"Hi Jack, feeling ok?" she asked, whilst working the machine.

I waved "All good, thanks to you"
"As long as you're ok" she said, and walked off holding two cups of coffee.
I looked at Steve.
"Yes, I've been chewed out for not telling her" he said.
"Ah, ok, makes sense now" I laughed.
"Fuck you, dickhead" he said "What you want?"
"Ah, and there he is!" I said to Kyle, who laughed.
"Funny. You want fucking lunch or something I suppose? Go sit, I'll go sort it"
I held up my hands in surrender "Ok, ok"
We went and found a table. My usual table was taken, so we went outside instead. It was pretty nice out, so we didn't really mind.
"Oh, it's nice to get some fresh air" Kyle said, sinking into his seat
"Yeah, it is" I said, doing the same.
We sat in silence for a while until Steve came out with our lunches. "Here you go fuckwads, enjoy"
He put the plates down and disappeared back inside. Kyle laughed; the old Steve was back. But I could sense something under the surface. I made a mental note to call him later to see what was up. Pushing the thought to one side, I ate my lunch.

I got home just after six, tired, and done for the day. A mild headache was lurking in the background, mostly from staring at a screen I guess. I needed to go get my eyes re-tested. Chrissy was curled up on the sofa watching some period drama or other. "Hey, how are you?" she asked as I sat next to her.
"Tired" I lay my head on her side, and she stroked my head till I fell asleep. She woke me up when her episode had finished.
"You want dinner?" she asked.
"Nah, I'm not hungry. I may just have some toast later" I said.
She ruffled my hair "Make sure you eat"

"Yes mum"
She started another episode, and I lay back down. I didn't sleep, but wasn't fully with it either. Thoughts going through my mind:
1. What was going on with Steve?
2. Was there something wrong with my head?
3. My kids.

The first one was easily answered; I just needed to call him.
The second not so easy…
The third; I got my phone out and started texting both of them.

Enthusiastic responses were received. They were doing well, and missed me loads.
It warmed my heart.
I thought that I hadn't made an appointment with the doc. I was sure Chrissy was going to ask about it, but she didn't. Mid way through the episode, I got up and said I was going to call Steve. I went out into the kitchen and dialled my friend's number.

"Hullo?"
"Hello. Thought I'd call and see what was going on" I said.
"Hmm, you know, stuff" he replied.
"Really? That's it? Stuff?"
"Well, I was told off by Willow which put me down a bit"
"That's it?"
"No"
"What's up mate?"
"Jazz"
Jazz? What? Oh. Shit.
"Fuck. Sorry mate, I'd forgotten" I said, apologetically.
"It's ok, I'd almost forgotten myself"
Today was the 7th anniversary of Jasmine's death. I felt like a dick. I'd forgotten. It was fading from my memory.

"Sorry"
"Like I said, I forgot too. That's probably why I feel so shit. It's fading from my memory already"
"It's probably what she'd want for you, you know that right?"
"Yeah, I know"
"It's been seven years. She'd be happy to know you're moving on with your life after all this time"
"You think?"
"I know. You think she'd want you mourning her for the rest of your life?"
"No, you're right. Of course you're right"
"She was a beautiful art of your life. Willow is your life now"
"Yeah she is"
"Make sure she knows"
"What?"
"You love her?"
"Of course I do"
"Marry her"
"What?"
"Marry the girl. She's carrying your child, you love her. What more do you need?"
"Hmmmm"
"Look, I know you don't like the thought, but you can't think that the same thing is going to happen"
"Yeah"
"She's further along than Jazz, and everything will be ok" I assured him
"You're right. Again"
"Marry her"
"I will"
"Soon"
"I'll go ring shopping at the weekend"
"Good lad. Make it romantic though will you for fuck sake"
"I will, don't worry"

"Good man"
"Hey Jack?"
"What?"
"Thank you"
"You're welcome. Now go make up with her"
"I will. Cheers mate"

I hung up. *Well done Jackie lad*. Thanks. I felt like I'd done something good, and it made me feel great.
Happy as a pig in shit, I made toast, then went back and lay with Chrissy till bedtime.

In bed, I did my usual and went over the day's events in my mind. The day had started shit. Really shit. But, I'd managed to turn things around. Steve was happy, I was happy, Kyle was happy, and I was sure Chrissy was happy. Or she would be when I made my appointment tomorrow.

I smiled to myself, put my headphones in, and drifted off to Victorian London for a rendezvous with danger. Awesome.

Day 4, Wednesday, 13th of June.

I woke to the sound of my alarm ringing in my brain. Ugh, too early surely. I checked; no mistake, it was 07.00. Yes, I have the luxury of sleeping till seven. I can hear most of you moaning that you're up far earlier than that. Well, good for you. I work like a three minute walk from my house. Do you?
Anyway. Yeah, I'm grumpy. I slept like a bag of shit. Don't know why, just did. Nothing particularly bad on my mind other than the fainting thing, so wasn't at all sure what had happened last night. I turned; Chrissy was already up. Unusual. I got up and went to find her.
Eh? Not downstairs. I looked in the office, nope. Where is she? Ah. In Elsie's bed. What had happened to make that happen?? Fuck. I felt guilty. I quietly went down to make her a nice breakfast to make up for whatever I'd done.
Hey.
What?
You know what you can do?
What?
Something that would make this a lot better.
Fuck sake, what? And it better not be X-rated
Tickets.
What?
Tickets dickhead.
What tickets?
Erm, Killers?
Fuck. Of course. I'd totally forgotten about those.
Welcome…
Thanks.
For once, I'd come up with a great idea.
Erm? Hello? That was me?

You're me, remember.
Touché.
I'd make a great breakfast and add the tickets to the deal. I knew she liked the band, so job's a good'n. Smugly, I went to work.

Tangent…

Imagine, it's been a few days since a tangent! Ok, so I realise the Killers never played in PB, but allow me some artistic licence here will ya? I was trying to think of a band I liked in about 2014, and they sprang to mind. I did originally have Arctic Monkeys, but I was kidding myself, especially after writing "I knew she liked the band" above; I was never a fan. Killers though…
So, wind yer neck in and get over it. (Killers did play in the UK in 2014, but at the V Festival)

Anyhoo, I could hear the shower running, and breakfast was on schedule to be finished when she was dressed. Good work. I set the table, and poured the coffee. I'd just put her plate on the table when she appeared. She looked tired. Fuck.
"Morning" she said, rubbed her eyes, then looked at the table. I'd made coffee, freshly squeezed oj, scrambled eggs à la James Bond, and toast.
"The fuck?" she looked at me, confused "Did I miss something?"
"I felt bad after noticing you'd slept in Elsie's room, so I made you breakfast"
Obviously not awake despite the shower, she picked up the envelope "What's this?"
"Open it"
She opened it and gasped "Jack what the fuck??" she jumped up and down with happiness.

She ran over and hugged me. "I should sleep in Elsie's room more often" she said. "I love the Killers!" She looked so happy, it was good to see. My shit mood from earlier was lifted instantly.

"Well, they're not really from me. I got them from Kyle as a thank you" I confessed.

"Doesn't matter" she said "Just what I needed. I had a terrible night"

And there it is… Shit. "I'm sorry"

"For what?" she asked, confused.

"For whatever I did to piss you off so much you left the room"

She shook her head "No, dummy. It wasn't you. It was me. I had such a restless shit night, and I knew I was keeping you awake, so I left to let you sleep"

Ah, that explains it. "Oh, I see. Well, regardless, sit and enjoy"

"Oh I will" she said, sitting down and rubbing her hands. "This looks yummy"

"Pity you don't deserve it" I said, taking the plate away.

"Hey! Don't make me shoulder punch you" she warned.

With a smile, I hastily put the plate back "Enjoy"

I left her to it, and went up to shower.

No run this morning?

Nah, I may do something in the office over lunch. No need to pack a bag; I had kit there. I got dressed, and went to get myself some breakfast.

"Here you go" Chrissy said as I walked into the kitchen I took the plate of toast and mug of coffee "I have a meeting to join, enjoy" she added, and went of upstairs. "Oh, and Jack?" she called down.

"Yes?"

"Make the doctor's appointment today please?"

"Will do" Fuck. How did she know I hadn't done it yet?

Probably because you would have told her about it if you had? Truth. What a woman. *Agreement.*

I finished my breakfast, and headed off to the office.

Tangent.

Scrambled eggs à la James Bond? Da fook?
The recipe was in a short story; 007 in New York. Just scrambled eggs really, but with a shit tonne of butter. Chrissy's guilty pleasure.
Yes, it's a thing. Look it up.

Back to reality. Kyle was busily working away when I walked in. "Morning Kyle"
"Morning Jack" he paused, clicked his mouse a few times, then looked up "How are you this morning?"
"I'm fine thanks, how are you?"
"Well, you know, so-so"
"Oh?" I could sense he wanted to expand and talk about something. Unusual for him, as he was the quiet type.
"Problems with the parents, you know" he said, waving his hand as if to dismiss the comment
"You want to chat about it?" I asked
"Nah, you have better things to do" he said, again dismissively.
"You're important Kyle, come on" I walked over to the small meeting table we had set up in the corner. He joined me, and looked nervous. "No need to be nervous Kyle, I'm just a friend, looking out for a friend"
"I know, it's a difficult subject though, you know?"
I had my suspicions, so agreed "I can imagine. If you don't want to talk about it its fine"
"No" he said, resolutely "I want to. It's so hard, I have nobody to talk to about it"
"You have Jas?"
"I know, but he's involved, so is biased. Does that make sense?"
"Sure. I have a feeling I know what it's about" I said.

"You do?"
"Parents?" I offered.
"Exactly" he said "They are convinced I'm not gay. Can you believe that?"
"Look, as a parent, let me give you the "Parental View". Here's what parents hope for when they have children; continuation of the family line. Sounds terribly old fashioned, but bear with ok?"
He grunted
"I know you think its bullshit, but let me finish. When you have kids, and when the grow up, there's something you look forward to more than anything"
"Grandkids"
"Yes, grandkids. It's kind of a guarantee that your family line will live on. Imagine for a second you have kids now. Would you be concerned that they were the last to bare your family name? Would you want them to have a family of their own?"
"I guess I'd want them to have their own family one day" he admitted
"Trust me, as you get older the whole family name thing will become more important, it's weird."
"Ok, I'll take your word for it" he said with a hint of a smile.
"I guess what I'm trying to say is this; give them some room to maneuver. They are trying to process the fact that they won't have grandkids"
"There's nothing saying I can't have kids, just because I'm gay. There are ways"
"I know that. But all they see is doom and gloom. You may be a man of the modern world Kyle, but they aren't. Trust me, the fact that its considered normal to be gay is a new phenomenon. And I mean that in the best possible way"
"I know that"

"Their generation, and the one before were not used to gay people being so accepted, if that makes sense? It was still a taboo for them"

He thought for a moment "You're right. Maybe I'm too hard on them. Will they ever change though?"

"I'm sure they will in time. You're their son, their only child. It's difficult, but you're going to have to live with it if you want to keep a relationship with them"

"I was so angry with them yesterday that I was tempted to break off all ties with them"

"I can understand that. I just hope you can see things a little from their perspective now"

He took a deep breath. "Yes, I think I can. Thank you Jack"

"Anytime partner, always here for you"

Wow, that was an intense start to the day! *Fuck aye, Jesus.*

The rest of the morning went pretty quickly; we went back to work, and resurfaced just after lunchtime. "How you getting on over there?" I asked.

"Got three big ones left"

"Wow, good effort. I have four, and a small one. Why don't you call it a day and go see your parents. Have a chat, with an open mind."

"You sure?" he asked.

"Of course. You're a partner now, you come and go as you please. As long as the work gets done, why should either of us care what hours we keep?"

"Thanks Jack" he shut down, and packed his laptop into his bag

"I'll have my laptop just in case you need me to do something"

I gave him a thumbs up, and he left. There was an instant silence in the office. I didn't like it. Time for a run. I got changed, put some music on, and jumped on the treadmill.

I was almost at my 5k mark when Chrissy walked into the office.

"Hey you" she smiled. I stuck up a finger, indicating I'd need a minute, so she sat at my desk.
"So this is where you hang all day huh?"
I finished the 5k, and shut down the treadmill "hang out?" I said, dripping with sweat
"Yes, hang. I know you, you love your work, and it's not a chore for you"
"You're right, I love it. And yes, this is where I hang all day" I winked "To what do I owe the pleasure?"
"Well, knowing you as I do, I also know for a fact that you haven't called the doctor yet" she said, with an accusatory squint.
"Guilty" I said. "Let me shower quickly, and I'll do it"
"Ok, I'll wait" she said smiling.
You sure you don't want to ask her to help out in the shower? No, but I'm not going to ask.
"Ask what?" She said, confused. *Lol, penis.*
"Oh, nothing" I said, and disappeared off to have a quick shower.
When I reappeared a few minutes later, she was still sat in my chair, browsing on her phone. She looked up "Ah, there you are. Here" she threw my phone over.
I rolled my eyes.
"Don't you roll your eyes at me old man, get on with it!"
I dialed the number, and spoke to the receptionist. After a brief chat, I hung up. "There. Happy?"
"When?" she asked
"Friday morning, half past ten"
She checked her phone "Super, I can come with"
I smiled "Awesome" *Did you mean that?* Of course I did. *Sure...*
"You can take me for lunch now" she said, and kissed me.
"Oh can I now?"
"Yes, you can. I'm starving"
I checked the time; it was almost half past one.

Instantly, my stomach groaned loudly.
"And you are too by the sounds of it" she laughed.
"Yeah, it would appear so" I said, laughing. I grabbed my phone, locked up, and took her for lunch.

"Where's Kyle today?" she asked as we walked through the village.
"He's taken the rest of the day to sort a family matter" I said.
"Oh?" I knew what that tone meant; *tell me now or I'll kill you*.
I told her what had happened the issues with his parents, and the chat we'd had this morning.
"Anyone ever told you that you'd make a great agony aunt?" she asked
"Not really" I said
"That was good advice, well done. It's hard for this generation to understand the mind-set of generations that came before them"
"Yeah, it is." I agreed
"They take everything for granted, and don't realise most of what they consider normal was considered abnormal or taboo by those before them"
"Well, he seemed to take it on board, and am hoping he's having a fruitful chat with his folks right now" I said as we walked up to the café.
"Wait" she said as I was about to open the door.
"What?"
"Come here" she took my hand and led me to the narrow alley between of the two rows of houses.
She took me in her arms, and kissed me deeply. "I love you Jack Beckett" she said when we came up for breath.
"I love you too Christelle Lenoir" I said. She kissed me again, and I was soon losing myself in a whirl of sexual tension.
"Whoa! Let's stop it there shall we" I said, breaking away.
 "Things are getting a bit too heated"

What? What the fuck are you doing??
She licked her lips and giggled.
"Stop it!" I said "Come on"
Can't believe what I'm hearing. Fucking hell.
Shut up.
I dragged her back out of the alley, and we went inside.

Tinkle

"Ello 'ello! What the fuck you two been up to?"
"What?" I asked, trying to look confused.
"Don't play innocent with me boyo, I saw you being dragged into the alley by that brazen hussy" he said waving his finger at Chrissy "And you're both all flushed" then he pointed his finger at me "And you have lippy all over your mouth"
Chrissy blushed, but not as much as I did. Fuck.
"Ah see! I was right! Get a fucking room already. Fuck sake"
What to do? Whilst Chrissy just giggled, I wasn't sure how to react. I knew he was only taking the piss, but it highlighted yet again the extreme sexual tension in our relationship. It was getting more and more difficult to either stop, or abstain. Not good. How far away was Florence? 11 days. Thank fuck. *What makes you think it's going to happen then?* I'm not actually sure, just a feeling. *Ah, well let's fucking well hope so!* We can agree on that.
"Agree on what?" Steve asked, puzzled. *Fucking hell you prick, sort it out!*
"We should get a room" I winked at Chrissy, she smiled, and went off to find Willow.
"She's not here today" Steve said.
"Oh?"
"She went to see her mum in London, back tomorrow. I'm closing up in a bit to go do some stuff" he winked at me. Ah, the ring. Good man.

"Oh, ok, we don't have to do lunch" I said winking.
"Nah, its cool, have a seat. Extra half hour won't kill me"
I stuck my thumb up, and went off into the garden terrace with Chrissy.
"That was funny" she giggled.
"Yeah it was, embarrassing, but funny. Felt like a guilty teenager"
"You going to tell me what the winking was all about" she said.
"What?"
"Wasn't a question, more of an order" she looked at me intensely.
"Wow, erm, I'm not…." I stammered, but she cut me off.
"Well?" Expectant look.
"Ugh. Ok. I told him to marry her" I said quietly.
"What?" she asked
"What? Not good?" I said, rather confused.
"No, brilliant" she beamed "Told you, you should be an agony aunt"
"You sure?"
"About the agony aunt? Of course"
"No you idiot, the marriage thing"
"Of course. They love each other, and she is carrying his child" she replied. "You did a good thing"
"He did?" Steve asked, walking out, oblivious of what we were talking about.
"Yeah, he did" Chrissy said, patting me on the back.
"Good for him" he said, putting the plates down. "Eat up and get out would you, I have things to do"
"We will" I assured him.
He walked off.
"Hey, Stephen" Chrissy called after him.
He stopped and turned "What?"
"Make it romantic won't you, for fuck sake?" she said.
"What the actual fuck…" he said, looking at me. *Uh-oh!*

I held up my hands and faked innocence.
"Don't look at him" she said "Female intuition" she winked.
"Fucking women" he muttered, and walked away.
"Female intuition?" I laughed.
"Well, you know, rather that, than you getting into trouble"
"Thank you" I leaned over and kissed her.
"Welcome, now let's eat and get out. I have the feeling we're outstaying our welcome…"
I agreed. We ate, helped clean up, and left a rather confused Steve to go off and do his thing.
What a woman. Absolutely.

I went back to the office, and a very happy Chrissy walked on back to the house to attend yet another meeting. The hours passed by far too quickly, and before I knew it, it was almost six. *Fucknation, call it a day would you?* Yeah, you're right. I saved my work, and secured the office.
When I got home, I found Chrissy on her phone in the living room.
"Hello" I said quietly.
"Hey you" she said louder than I had expected "What? No not you, you muppet. Send me some pictures and I'll have a look"
She dialled off, and put her phone down. A few seconds later it buzzed repeatedly.
"Client? Muppet?" I said.
"Stephen" she said. "Ring shopping"
"Ah"
"Sit" she said, patting the sofa.
I sat next to her, and she showed me the pictures Steve had sent of the rings he was considering.
"Wow"
"Yeah, wow. Some of them are a bit much though aren't they?" she said.
"You think? I thought women loved diamonds?"

"If you pay attention, you'd notice that Willow doesn't wear a lot of jewellery. She has one very plain necklace she wears that she got from her parents"

"Ah, hadn't noticed"

"I know. Men tend not to. To me, that says, she's not going to like anything to glamorous."

She flicked through the pictures "This one is perfect" she said. This ring she had singled out was fairly plain; platinum with a medium sized diamond mounted in it. It looked classy.

"You're right. It's lovely" I agreed.

She text Steve, telling him as much. "There, done" she put her phone down. "Now, where were we?" she said, leaning in.

"No, no, no" I said, pushing her away. *Yes, yes, yes dickhead*. No!

"Ok, I get the picture" she said "No need to shout"

"Sorry, inner monologue, you know…"

"Inner voice says yes right?" she winked.

"Yes, it does"

"I love you inner voice!" she shouted in my ear. *Fuck yeah! What a woman!*

"Fuck sake, I'm not deaf" I said, rubbing my ear "Don't encourage it"

She giggled.

"What are we doing for dinner?" I asked, changing the subject.

"Oh, I don't know. I'm not really that hungry"

"Me neither. Fancy a pint though…"

"Come on then" she said, getting up "Bar it is"

We went out to the bar in the garden, and enjoyed a few beers whilst playing some great music.

Only a couple mind. School night innit.

Later on, I lay in bed going through the days' events. Wow, quite a lot had happened today. I hadn't heard anything form Kyle, but was sure I'd find out tomorrow.

Steve was happy; he had bought the ring and was busy planning how he would propose. Somewhere in the depths of my brain, there was a dim spark. Couldn't make it out, but I'm sure it would come to me eventually.

In the meantime, I put my headphones in and just about made it to Paddington station to catch the train. I found Holmes and Watson in a first class compartment, discussing the case they were working on. I nodded to each in turn, and took a seat next to Dr Watson.

Day 5, Thursday, 14th of June.

Buzz Buzz!
??
Buzz Buzz!
Wtf?
Groggily, I picked up my phone; messages and missed calls from Steve.
Answer the phone you wanker!
Shit. I focused, and dialed his number. He answered immediately.

"The fuck?" He sounded upset.
"Mate, sorry I was asleep"
"Never mind that, Willow is in hospital"
"What?"
"Get your ass over here, I need a lift"
"On way"
I threw the phone down, and woke Chrissy.
"Hey, wake up, something is wrong"
"What?" she said, half a sleep and confused.
"Willow is in hospital. Come on"
"Fuck!" she jumped out of bed and started changing. I did the same, and a few minutes later we were in the car on the way to Steve's house.
"Did he say what was wrong? Not the baby!" Her voice full of worry.
"Didn't say. I fucking hope not"
We pulled up outside Steve's to find him stood on the pavement, waiting for us.

"Royal Free Hospital" he blurted out as he got in "M1, then A41, I'll direct you"
I put the car into gear, and sped off towards our destination.
"The fuck is going on?" I asked.
"Please tell me it's not the baby" Chrissy added desperately.
"I don't know" he replied "I just had a call from her mum saying she'd been rushed in"
The drive should have taken around 1 hour 40, but we made it in just over an hour. It was 03.15, and the roads were dead, thankfully.
I let Steve out at the front door "Go. I'll park and find you"
Chrissy jumped out with him, and they both ran inside. Finding a space at three in the morning wasn't hard, and I was sat with Chrissy a few minutes later. "They said anything yet?" I asked, sitting down.
"Not to me, Steve is with her now"
"Fucking hell, please don't let there be a problem with the baby. Not after last time" I said
"Hey, it'll be fine" Chrissy said, trying to comfort me, but it wasn't working.
"What if it happens again? What if…"
"Hey!" she said sharply "Not going to happen. Ok?"
With that, Steve came out. "What's not going to happen?" We both jumped to our feet
I looked at him "Nothing"
"I know what you're thinking, but she's ok. They're both ok" he beamed. "She was bleeding quite a bit, but everything is ok"
"Oh thank fuck" Chrissy and dropped back into her chair.
I hugged him. "That's good to hear mate"
"I know. I was fucking terrified" he said, and started to cry.
"Hey, it's all good now right?" I said.
"Yeah, but you know. I thought it was happening again"
"But it isn't." I said "It isn't"
He nodded "Yeah, I know"

"Good" I patted his back "She needs you mate"
We separated, and Chrissy asked "Did they say what it was?"
"Bleeding during pregnancy is normal. She just bled more than is normal, so they brought her in just to be sure"
"I'm glad everything is ok" She gave him a quick hug.
"Thanks guys, I appreciate you bringing me"
"No problem" I said "That's what friends are for right?"
Again, he nodded. "I appreciate it. I'm staying here, you guys go home to bed. I'll let you know how things are going"
You sure?" Chrissy asked.
"Yeah, go. There's nothing to be done, she's getting discharged in the morning. She'll be staying with her mum for a bit, then I'll pop down and pick her up when she's ready to come home"
"If you're sure" I said.
"Yep, sure, go. Get home" He waved us away.
"Ok mate. You let me know how it's going though ok?" I said.
"Will do"
We said our goodbyes, and left a very relieved Steve behind. The drive home was mostly in silence, and Chrissy fell asleep about twenty minutes into the drive. I got us home safe, and we went to bed. It was 05.57. Seemed pointless going to bed. I text Kyle t let him know I'd be late in. I needed sleep.

Sleep didn't come. I was awake till the alarm went off at eight. We'd afforded ourselves a bit of a lay in, as Chrissy had no meetings till after nine. She was woken by the alarm, and possibly the smell of fresh coffee on her bedside table. "Och, wow" she complained as she silenced the alarm "Already?"
She saw the coffee and turned "Did you sleep at all?"
"No, I had memories of Jasmine going through my head"
She sat up and kissed my head "Poor thing. I can't even imagine how Steve was feeling"
"I can" Having lived through the whole ordeal with them, I knew exactly how he felt.

"Thank you for the coffee" she said, picking up the mug and taking a sip "You're very considerate, you know that?"
"Yeah, I know"
"And ever so modest" she laughed.
"I'm a parent, it's what we do"
She leaned in and fluttered her eyes "You want me to call you daddy?"
"Good god no" I said, pushing her away "That's creepy as fuck"
She laughed "You're very conservative Beckett"
"I'm old fashioned, and I make no apologies for it" I said in mock disgust.
"It's part of what makes me love you" she said seriously, and kissed me "I have to get up, meeting at nine" She finished her coffee and disappeared off to the bathroom. I'd showered before I made her coffee, so got up and dressed. I didn't want Kyle to think I was tasking the piss.
I knocked on the bathroom door "I'm just off to my appointment, see you later"
"Ok, love you" came the response.
"Love you too, bye"

My session with Pam was good. We talked a lot about my inner fears, after I told her about what had happened with Willow. She said it was natural to harbour these deep-seeded, primal fears. Even if they weren't related to yourself. I felt much better for having our chat. She was more concerned with the fainting episodes, as they seemed to be getting more frequent, and was relieved to hear I'd made a doctors' appointment for tomorrow. I told her I'd let her know how it went. All too soon, the session was over, and I found myself back in the village, walking to the office. Gave Steve a call as I walked to see how things were going. All was well. Thank fuck.
They would be leaving the hospital as soon as she could get discharged, then would go to her mother's house.

He wasn't opening the caff today, sorry. I told him not to be an idiot, the caff wasn't going anywhere.

The conversation put a smile on my face; I was happy.

I got to the office to find Kyle hard at work. Don't know what else I was expecting to see; the kid was conscientious.

"Morning" he said as I walked in "You ok?"

"Yep, I'm good ta. You?"

"All good"

Short. To the point. Very Kyle. "So, I had an interesting morning" I said.

"Oh?" he replied, turning towards me

I told him all about what had happened, and how tired I was.

"Wow, that's both terrible and amazing" he said, and got up. "I'll get you a coffee"

"Thanks mate" I said, and opened the post. "Hey, hey"

"What?"

"The forms are here" I said, waving a pack of papers in the air.

"Forms?"

"Partnership forms"

"Oh, wow"

"My, no, *our* solicitor is coming at ten to go through them and hopefully to get you to sign"

"Hopefully?" he asked.

"Well, you know, you may change your mind"

"Not likely" he said with a smile.

He's a funny sausage, and I was glad he hadn't changed his mind. Things would be much better as partners. After all; he was the one with the brains and ability, I was just the old guy plodding along. In other words, he was the future. I was happy about the partnership, I liked giving somebody a future.

A secure future as it would turn out. But, for the moment, we sat and chatted about it, as he had a lot of questions. Seeing him happy made my day, and I soon forgot all about my exhaustion.

After seeing what his wage was going up to, he started talking excitedly about getting a mortgage so they could move out of their rented flat in PB. They wanted to move somewhere quieter like Whittlesey or Chatteris.
"Chatteris?" I asked.
"Yeah, is small and quiet, but not too small. If that makes sense"
"It's a lovely place" I assured him.
"I can't wait to start looking for a place of our own" he said, super excited.
"I'm sure you'll find somewhere perfect for the two of you"
"Thanks Jack" he stood and hugged me "You have no idea what this means"
"Oh, I can imagine" I laughed.
At the time, I wondered why a young couple would want to move away from the vibrant nightlife, to a quiet little village. I had no idea of the abuse they had suffered in the city because of their sexuality, he only told me about it years later. It had been quite horrible, and I was glad they got out.

Tangent?

Don't know what on, but it seems light on tangential musings to this point.
You have kids? Did you go through something like Willow? I can tell you, it's the scariest thing in the world. And that's speaking from experience. Anything happens that's abnormal is terrifying, and you immediately fear the worst.

Also, are you wondering why I would make Kyle an equal partner? Why give away half of my business? I'm not a stupid person; I'm not super quick with this kind of stuff. Kyle is a whizz kid however, and is all over it.
Business is growing rapidly, and I'm not going to be able to keep up.

However, I can't just quit either; I have a mortgage, child support, and a pension to pay for. This for me was the easiest way, as I could still do all that, and gradually scale down my input. Possibly even take on someone else. As it turned out, Kyle had no objections to me scaling down my input over the years, as it was my company after all. I was lucky to have him.

Kids? Yep, still alive. They'll be coming tomorrow, don't worry.
Parents? Also still alive. We'll be seeing them tomorrow too.
Cat? Still going strong, spends most of the time sleeping on the bar roof.
Anything else Doctor? Tomorrow morning remember…
Let's get back…

Yes, I was lucky to have him. I checked my watch; just after nine. We had some time before Geoff got here, so I immersed myself into a video edit. A short one, of course.
I was dragged out of my little work universe by Kyle snapping his fingers in my face. "Earth to Jack?"
"What? Oh, hey, sorry"
"It's cool" he laughed "Mr. Baines is here"
"Morning Jack" Geoff said, stood behind Kyle.
"Shit, sorry Bainsey, I was lost in work there"
He laughed "No worries mate, whenever you're ready."
I stood "Coffee?"
"Tea if you have it" he responded.
"Of course, make yourself at home" I went over to the small kitchenette and put the kettle on "White none, right?"
"Yep" Geoff set up camp at the small conference table. Kyle came up to me and said "I'm nervous, stupid right?"
"Not at all, you may be nervous now, but you'll be happy in a bit"
"I guess that's true"

I handed him the cup of tea "Here, take this, go introduce yourself to Geoff, relax."
He wandered over to where Geoff was sat, and I popped out to the loo.
When I got back, they were chatting amiably. Result. I knew Kyle wasn't much of a talker, and this was going to be difficult for him, but he was doing himself proud.
I knew this was going to take while, so I made a coffee for Kyle and myself before I joined them.
"Right" Geoff said when I'd taken my seat "Shall we begin?"
Big smiles all round.
We got to work. It was a lengthy process, as we had to line by line the entire document, so Kyle understood exactly what he was getting into. Geoff had to explain quite a lot of the business jargon, but was extremely patient, which put Kyle at ease. It was a lot to get his head around, particularly because he had no previous experience, or qualifications in business studies. It was a lot to take in, but he was a smart guy and dong well. By the time it we were ready to sign on the dotted line, it was almost one o'clock.
"You sure you're happy?" I asked Kyle as he picked up the pen.
He didn't need time to think "I'm happy" he said, and signed.
"Ok, as long as you are, I am" I said, and signed my name.
"Excellent, all done then. Congratulations Kyle" Geoff said, smiling. He held out his hand, and Kyle shook it with confidence.
"Thank you Mr. Baines" he beamed.
"Please, it's Geoff" he insisted "or Bainsey if you must" he added with a wink.
"Excellent" I smiled "We should celebrate"
"And that's my cue to leave" Geoff smiled "Thank you gentlemen, good to see you Jack" he said shaking my hand
"And nice to meet you Kyle, congrats again" they shook hands.
"Have a great day gents" he picked up his stuff, and left.

"Thanks Bainsey, catch up soon" I called after him. He held up a hand in acknowledgment.

The office was quiet for a minute. "You ok?" I asked.

"Yep, I'm great" Kyle smiled "I'm just taking it all in"

I patted him on the back "Plenty of time for that partner, let's go get lunch"

As the café was shut, we had to make do with lunch in the pub. Fucking hardship right…

Fuck yeah! Let's get smashed!

Oh, you're still here then?

Of course Jackie boy, just biding my time, you know…

No I don't, but ok…

The pub was very busy, as expected. All the locals had to go here instead of the caff for lunch. Good business for the pub. We managed to find a small table towards the back, and sat down.

"Wow, busy in here" Kyle said.

"Café is shut, so they've nowhere else to go" I winked.

"Oh yeah. How is everything?" he asked

"All good, I spoke to Steve this morning, Willow is good, and getting discharged" I checked my phone "Correction, has been discharged, and at her mums with a cup of tea"

"Excellent news"

"Right" I said "Let's order. You fancy a pint?" I asked.

"Work?" he said, a bit unsure.

"We are the executives, let's vote. All those in favour?" I stuck up my hand, but was slower than Kyle. I smiled "Good man. I think we're on track to finish tomorrow right?"

"Yes, we are" he nodded.

"Good, then let's enjoy our afternoon"

And we did. After our burger and pint lunch, we had a few more jars to celebrate our new partnership. When I say a few, I mean a lot. Kyle exploded into life after pint no.5, and we had a great afternoon playing tunes on the jukebox and having a right old laugh. It's a cherished memory, even now.

Towards dinner time, I put Kyle in a taxi, and he disappeared off home. I was a bit unsteady on my feet. I hadn't felt too bad inside, but out here in the fresh air, I was wobbling noticeably.
Lol, good effort lad, proud of you!
Thanks, I enjoyed it.
Ok, now you just have to get us home with minimum embarrassment.
Hmm, easier said than done… I put out an arm to steady myself against a wall. Let's rest for a sec. *Rest? You've walked like 10 yards you fucking penis.*
Shhhhh…
"You ok there son?"
Like an absolute superhero, my dad appeared at the right time. "Dad" I smiled.
"Out walking the dog. Looks like you've had a good afternoon eh?" he said laughing. "Come on, let's get you home"
He took my arm, and walked me to the house. "What you been doing?" he asked
"Celebrating" No shit dickhead…
"Celebrating?"
"I made Kyle a partner in the business, we had a couple to celebrate"
"More than a couple it looks like" dad laughed.
"Yeah, maybe just a few more" I giggled.
"We're here" he said, and rang the bell.
Chrissy opened the door. "Whoa! What happened here?" she laughed, looking at the state of me.
"Found this staggering through the village" dad joked
"Thought I'd return it to its owner"
"Thank you" Chrissy said "Not sure it's mine though"
"Eh?" I managed "Of course I am" Things were a bit fuzzy. You need to lay down asap partner, let's sleep this off. No truer word had ever been spoken.

"Come on you bum, let's get you in" she helped dad get me to the sofa, and dropped me like a brick. I was out almost as soon as I landed.

"What's he been doing?" Chrissy asked.

"Celebrating with Kyle" dad explained.

"Ah, partner day. Gotcha"

"He'll be ok, just needs to sleep it off" dad said "Want to join me for a walk?"

Chico engaged tail waggle as if on cue… "How could I resist?" Chrissy said, ruffling the dogs head.

Darkness.
Rotation.
Nausea.
Increasing rotational speed…
No, please don't.
Jack!
Stop spinning!
Jack!
What?
Get to the toilet. Now.
Good idea.
I made it just in time, and the contents of my stomach erupted as soon as I embraced the loo.
Oh my god…
That's what you get you dick.
Thanks stomach. Sleep…
Yeah, thanks stomach, you prick. Erm, Jack?
Zzzzzzzz…
Jack?
Zzzzzzzz…
Holy fuck. Here? Sigh…
I was blissfully off in the land of z's. Until a violent rocking sensation hit me.

"Fuck sake, not again" I mumbled. *Yeah, fuck off stomach, we're asleep!*

More rocking, slow motion sound of someone saying my name… Slowly, the sound caught up in tempo until I heard it clearly "Jack! Fuck sake, wake up"

Chrissy was shaking me. "Seriously? You fell asleep hugging the fucking toilet?"

"What?" Grog. Haze. Sleep required.

"Come on you idiot, let's get you to bed. You going to be sick again?"

I did a quick check; *Nope, I'm empty now, carry on.* "No"

"Good. Fuck sake, it stinks in here" She dragged me to my feet, and helped me back to the sofa. *Proud moment Jack lad, proud moment…*

Fuck you. This was your idea…

"Stay here" she said as she lay me down.

No problem there, I thought, and was out like a light.

Booting up mainframe…

Boot sequence complete.

My brain sent the signal to open my eyes. And again. And again. Until slowly, my eyelids responded.

Light seeped in. Ok, send focus command. Yo! Respond! Execute! Slowly, again, my eyes focussed. I looked around. It was dark outside. There was a glass of water. Drink! Please drink! My brain shouted. Is that a washing up bowl? Fuck me, you're in trouble. I moved my head, and slowly sat up.

"Hey, you're back" Chrissy said, smiling. She was sat on the other sofa watching telly. "How's the head?"

Quick system check: *We're in excruciating pain you fucking moron! Hydrate immediately!*

"Banging" I said.

"Water and ibuprofen there" she nodded to the table. *She is our saviour! We love her!*

I swallowed the pills and downed the contents of the glass. *Ah, things will be ok. Stand down from red alert!*

"Sorry" I said, unsure of the mood.

"No problem" she smiled "That must have been quite the celebration"

"I think it was that, and the euphoria of Willow being ok" *Wow, that's a big word considering the state you're in!*

"Bless. I cleaned up the loo, in case you were wondering"

"Ah. Yes. Erm, thanks" I said apologetically.

"You may want to brush your teeth" she said fanning her hand "Your breath is ripe"

Ugh. She was right. My mouth tasted like a horse had shit in it. *Smells like it too!*

Slowly, I got up. *Steadiness check… Good to go.* I made my way upstairs and brushed my teeth.

I checked myself in the mirror after. *Fucking hell, you look like shit.* Truth. I couldn't remember the last time I'd been sick after drinking. Let alone the last time I'd fallen asleep hugging a toilet. No wait, I can. Blackpool, 1991, Yates's wine lodge. The bouncer had to break open the door to get me out. I then fell asleep on the top deck of the tram in the cold and pissing down rain, going back to the B&B. Needless to say, I haven't touched a Bacardi and Coke since… (Writer speaking; True story! Thanks Cousin George!)

Where was I? Ah yes. Mirror.

I looked like shit. *I said that already!*

I felt like shit. *Yep, sure do.*

I took a deep breath. Wow, ok, time to get yourself together. I checked my watch; 20.43. Wtf?

Jack?

What?

You smell like shit.

Ugh, you're right. I stripped off and got in the shower.

Yeay! Hydration drench!
Just before I got out, I turned off the hot water. *Holy fuck! Why???* It was exhilarating.
My god that felt good. I was awake.
I dried off, put my pj's on, and went down to apologise to my girlfriend.
Girlfriend? What are you, like 12?
What do you mean? She is my girlfriend?
Penis, whatever. You gave that idiot Steve good advice
Hey, he's not an idiot. He's our best friend.
Truth. Apologies. Anyways, take your own advice.
The fuck you talking about?
MARRY HER!
Eh?
Marry the girl.
That stopped me in my tracks, half way down the stairs.
Marry her?
Yeah. Why the fuck not?
I hadn't even thought about it.
You love her?
Obviously
She love you?
Yes.
Do it.
Now?
No you muppet, how about on this shagging holiday you're going on?
Shagging holiday?
Yeah, you know it…
Ok, yeah, I do.
Wouldn't it be the icing on the cake?
You're making sense.
Of course I am. Buy a ring, propose in Italy.
I will.
Good lad.

Thanks.

"Thanks?" Chrissy said, standing at the bottom of the stairs, looking up at me. "You ok there?"

"Hmmm? Yeah, I'm ok" I said, and walked down to her. "I'm so sorry" I said "Don't know what happened"

"No need to be sorry. I'm just happy to see you happy. We all deserve happiness Jack"

Wait, is that a hidden message? Does she know? *Did you say it out loud you tosser?*

I was sure I hadn't.

"Thanks, I'm lucky to have you"

"Yes you are. You hungry?"

"Not really" Cue brain and stomach in unison: *We want toast you knobber!* "But, I guess I should have something. Toast?"

"Sit, I'll get you some" she said, pointing at a chair. I sat.

"I take it Kyle is in a similar state as you?"

"Dunno, possibly. I put him in a taxi" He had been very worse for wear; talking absolute bollocks, and just having a super time. Good lad, he needed a release.

"Hmmm, judging by the state you were in, I'd say it was a sure bet" she said "Here"

Toast! Rejoice! I ate greedily.

"Thought you weren't hungry?" she laughed.

"I guess I was" I smiled.

"You wanna cuddle up on the sofa and watch a bit of telly before bed?"

I didn't need to be asked twice "Yep"

As expected, I fell asleep. My head in her lap, her hand playing with my hair. Bliss.

She woke me around eleven, and we went to bed.

No need for headphones; I zonked out immediately.

Day 6, Friday, 15th of June.

I woke about half an hour before the alarm, crept out of bed, and went for a quick run. The cold morning air felt good in my lungs, bringing life to my tired body. I only ran 3k, just enough to wake me up. I returned home just as the sun was peeking through the bedroom windows. Chrissy was in the kitchen making a cup of tea. "Morning you, want tea?"
I kissed her "No thanks, I'm jumping in the shower"
"Ok. Want me to join?"
I came to a screeching halt. "What?"
She winked "Go on, I'll make you some breakfast"
Shit. Thought she meant it! Me too...
Today was a happy day. Kids were coming. I felt in a better place mentally after my chat with Pam, but was still a bit nervous about seeing the doc today. I had a quick shower, and got dressed. Chrissy came up, and said "Breakfast is on the table, don't forget the appointment at ten"
"I won't" I said, kissed her, and went down to eat. Scrambled eggs on toast, coffee. What a woman. *Yeah, aint she just...*
I had breakfast and went to the office. I was surprised to find Kyle already hard at work when I walked in. "Wow, morning mate" I said
"Morning Jack. How's the head?"
"A bit fragile, but ok" I said "You?"
"Hmmm, was bad last night, but ok at the moment"
"It was worth it though right?" I asked
"Yeah, totally" he smiled.
"Good. No then, what we got?" I sat, flashed up my system, and got to work. Chrissy walked in at 09.30 to pick me up for my appointment. "You ready?"
"Yep, two secs" I saved, and turned off the monitor. "Ready"

Kyle looked up "Good luck, hope all is ok"
"I'm sure it will be, thanks mate" I gave him a thumbs up.
"Hi Kyle" Chrissy smiled "Looking ok considering"
"Oh, yeah, erm…" the kid was embarrassed.
"Leave him alone" I said jokingly.
"Good to see you Kyle, congrats" she kissed his cheek, and he blushed even more.
"Wow, see what you've done now?" I said and dragged her out. She just giggled.

The drive to the doc's only took a couple of minutes, and we took a seat in the crowded waiting room. "Wow, busy today" I said as we sat.
A short time later, the doc popped his head out "Jack?"
I smiled, stood, and walked in, Chrissy in tow.
"You mind if Chrissy sits in?" I asked.
"If you don't, I don't" he said, shaking my hand.
Chrissy pulled up a chair, and sat with me.
"So, Jack, what can I do for you?"
"The fainting is getting more frequent" I said "I'm concerned there may be more to it"
"Our friend found him out cold on the canal bridge the other morning" Chrissy chimed in.
"That is concerning. You're not driving anymore I hope?" he asked.
"Nope, I have a personal chauffeur" I said looking at Chrissy
"Ah I see, well, that's probably for the best eh"
"I don't drive a lot anyway to be fair, I work in the village, so don't really need to"
"Good. Now then, let's have a look at you, over here please" he walked over to the patient table in the corner. "Sit, relax" he said, and took my blood pressure. "A bit low Jack, could be a touch of hypo-tension"
"Would that cause fainting?" Chrissy asked.

"Certainly, and other things besides if left untreated" he sat, and thought for a moment.
"Here's what I want you to do, buy a blood pressure monitor from the receptionist, and fill out this form for a week. Drop it in at reception any time. I'll check it. If your pressure stays low, you come back immediately. If it settles, I'll have you in for a chat anyway. Deal?"
"Sounds easy enough" I said.
"What if it stays low?" Chrissy asked "Can it be treated?"
"Of course, I can prescribe something to get it back up. But you can also make small changes to your lifestyle"
"Like what?" I asked.
"I know you're a runner, so no need to increase exercise. Eat smaller meals, more often, have a bit of salt with each meal. Not a lot, just a bit. And try not to sit for too long. Get a standing desk"
"Standing desk?" I asked.
"Yep, you can raise it up and stand at your workstation instead of sitting." he explained.
"Ok, I'll check it out"
"Excellent. Here's a couple of sheets" he said, handing me some paper "Go see Julia on the way out for the monitor, it's only a tenner"
"Will do, thanks doc" I stood and shook his hand.
"Good to see you Jack, and you Chrissy. Take care"
We left the surgery, monitor in hand, and drove home.
Nurse Lenoir busily explained how she was going to do the monitoring with me. It was almost like she didn't trust me. *She probably doesn't, you fuckbag.*
She dropped me off at the office, and I promised I would take a measurement after lunch.

When I got in, I gave Kyle a quick run-down on my appointment, then asked about stand up desks.

"We have those in college" he said "they're pretty awesome"
"Let's get some. Find one you like, and buy two" I said.
"Will do" he smiled.
"Excellent. Right, I have 2 vids to finish, then I'm off. How you getting on?" I asked.
"I'm basically done. I've just emailed off the last of my work. You want me to take one of yours?"
"Nah, its fine, I can get them done before five."
"Sure? I don't mind. I have nothing else planned today"
"Only if you're sure" I said "I don't want you thinking I'm taking the piss"
"Not at all, send me one over"
"Ok, thank you" I selected the smaller of the two and sent it over to him.
"Cool, I'll get on it now" he sat back down and went to work. I did the same.

Obviously, he finished before I did, and left to go home. I thanked him for helping out, and wished him a good weekend.
Ok, almost done, about an hour left. Get back to it Jack. I buckled down and got on with it.
Just over an hour later, I was done. I sent it off, checked email, and shut down. Boom. Done. It was 14.17; I had time before the kids got here. I locked up, and went home. Yes, the bp monitor is in my bag…

As soon as I got through the door, my private nurse accosted me to note down my readings. I dutifully provided my results, and she noted them on the chart. "Still low Beckett" she noted "Did you eat?"
"Eat?"
"I'll take that as a no then" she shook her head in disapproval.
"Sorry, trying to get used to it" I offered in my defence.

"Never mind, I'll make sure you do for the rest of the weekend" she smiled.

Joy.

"How you doing up here?" she touched my head. The feeling was like an electrical charge going through my body. *Whoa! What was that??*

"Erm, yeah, ok I think" I said, still shaken by the sensation.

"You sure? You look shaken"

"The sensation of your touch" I said.

"Fuck off" she responded "Don't take the piss"

"I wasn't" I said, deadpan.

"Oh" she didn't know what to say. Another one of those rare moments where she had been stunned into silence by compliment.

"Anyhoo" I said, saving her "I need to make sure the place is ready for the kids"

"Oh, yeah, sure. No, wait, I did it already"

"You did?"

"Yeah, cleaned and hoovered rooms, cleaned bathroom and toilets. All good."

"Oh" My turn to be stunned into silence. "Thank you" I kissed her.

"All we need to do is shopping" She said.

"We'll do that after, if you don't mind. The kids quite like shopping, and it gives me a rare opportunity to spoil them"

"Sounds like a plan Beckett"

"Is there anything I can do?" I asked, feeling a bit useless. "I finished early to get that stuff done"

"Well, there is one thing…" she said, winking. *Fuck aye!* I squinted "Yes..?"

"Go for a run with me? It's been a while"

"Oh, yeah, of course. Erm, sure" I blushed.

"You're a fruitcake Beckett, I don't always think about sex you know. Most of the time, but not all of it" she winked.

Oh my god. I LOVE this woman! Of course you do…
"Come on, let's get changed. Promise I won't look. Much"
We went off upstairs, changed into our running kit (with a few sneaky peeks both sides) and went out for a run. *She's fucking tidy.* Yeah, she is.
"Tidy?" she asked "Thanks"
Whoa!
Didn't know how to respond, so I didn't at all. We started our watches and set off towards the bridge and canal path. I need to get my mind under control. *Yes you fucking well do!*
The run was great, and we made it back with plenty of time for showers etc. before the kids arrived.
Naturally, I was super excited. I missed them so much.

Tangent. If I may. Not that you get a choice.

I miss my kids. Oh my god, I missed them so much. It was painful. I don't mention it, but there would be nights where I would just be crying in bed before falling asleep. Night time is bad; it gives you too much time to think. I know I always say I go through the days' events before I go to sleep, but this isn't part of that. This comes after. When the lights are out and its silent. It's dangerous. Hence the headphones.
Do you think your ex cares about the fact that you miss your kid(s)? I've often wondered. And then, as the years go by, do you think they care about the fact that you've missed out on 70% of your kid(s) lives? 70%.
(If you only see them 2 days a week) Think about that. You miss all the school stuff, helping with homework or problems. You miss all the personal stuff; watching TV together, playing games, just watching them grow up, etc.
After seven years, you'll have missed out on five years of their lives. 5 fucking years!!!

Holy fuck. And seven years flies by, believe me. That's time you'll NEVER get back. Before you know it, if you're not careful, you know very little about your own kid(s).
It's soul destroyingly fucking shit. And fucking aggravating. Grrrr.

"You ok there?" Chrissy asked.
"Hmm? Oh, yeah. Just thinking about how much I miss them"
We were sat out in the garden chilling out. I hadn't realised I'd drifted off into my own thoughts.
She put her arms around me "I know you do my love, and its shit. I know it is"
I was trying hard not to cry.
"You have to keep it together though ok? They'll be here soon"
"Yeah, I know, I'll be ok" I took a deep breath. "Ok, yeah, I'm fine"
"Good. It's important to talk about it. Never be afraid to ok?"
"I won't, thank you" *I'll make sure of it.* Thanks.
A few minutes later, the front door opened, and my heart was whole again. I held my kids for a while, just enjoying having them in my arms, having them close.
"Dad, you *can* let go you know?" Elsie said I laughed, and let her go. James didn't complain, because he didn't want to live with his mum. Things weren't good between them, but there wasn't much I could do.
"Sorry, I just missed you guys"
"We missed you to dad" James said "It's good to see you" he hugged me again. I stroked his head.
"It's good to see you too buddy"
I looked over at Chrissy; she had a tear in her eye. I raised an eyebrow, and she just waved her hand in dismissal, and composed herself.
She didn't have much time to do so, as Elsie was all over her.
"Hello you, I've missed you" she said, lifting her up.

"I missed you too" Elsie laughed.
Even James went in for a quick hug "Hi Chrissy"
"Hey James, great to see you"
We had a great time chatting about all the stuff we'd missed out on during the last two weeks.
Two fucking weeks! Jesus. Imagine not seeing your kids for two weeks. (Bliss for some I know)
We heard all about their trip to their Aunts, but very little about school. Standard. I knew they were doing well. If they weren't Helen would have told me. *She would?* Well, I'd like to think so at least.
Chrissy was joining without problems, and I was proud of my kids for accepting her so easily. It was my greatest concern, and I had some doubts, particularly with Elsie. But, they'd both done me proud.
"Hate to break up this perfect moment" I said "But we need to go shopping if you guys want to eat"
As expected, this made both kids happy "Yeay! Shopping!"
"Where are we going?" James asked.
"Erm…" I looked at Chrissy.
"Tesco in Chatteris" she said swiftly. Of course, I'd forgotten where we had decided to shop these days after a couple of uncomfortable run-ins. It was the only safe place to go these days.
"Let's hope we don't see anyone we know" I winked.
"Don't jinx it!" she laughed.
The kids looked confused, and it could stay that way; I wasn't going to tell them about our run-ins…
"Come on then" I said, throwing the keys over to Chrissy "You can drive". The kids didn't question, they just ran out to the car.

As it happened, we saw nobody we knew. It was great.
The kids ran around throwing random stuff in the trolley.
"Oi you two! What are you throwing in?" I asked jokingly.

"Just a few bits daddy" Elsie smiled.
I smiled. How could I possibly say no? "Ok my love"
We got the food for the weekend, and a pile of whatever the kids wanted. I noticed they put some school stuff in. I thought Helen was buying whatever they needed for school. *You're certainly giving her enough fucking money!* Truth. I was. *Oh well, put it out of your mind Jackie boy, just buy it.* You're right. I pushed the thought out, and carried on shopping.
I don't really want to talk about how much it cost! Let's just say it cost a small fortune.
Worth it though, the kids were happy, and that's all that mattered. *Truth.*
Chrissy gave James the car keys as we were laden with bags. He ran ahead and opened the boot for us.
"Thank you James" Chrissy said, and we loaded the bags in the car. The drive back was a happy one, with the kids going through their stuff in the back. We got back just after six, and they both disappeared upstairs with their stuff, leaving the grownups to deal with the shopping. We put the stuff away, and I put the kettle on.
"Oh, yes please" Chrissy said, tea would be lovely.

A few minutes later, we were sat outside, enjoying a nice cup of tea. And a few choc hob-knobs each. *Oh yeah, nice.*
"What's for dinner?" Chrissy asked.
"Not sure" I answered.
"I'll throw something together" she said.
"You sure?"
"Yeah, you go spend time with the kids"
"Thank you" I kissed her
"I know how much you've missed them, so go be with them"
I went up and knocked on James's door.
"Come in" he said from the other side.

"Hey mate" I said, and sat down on his bed "Just wanted to see how things were going at your mums"

His face dropped noticeably. "That good eh?"

"Dad, I just want to move here. Why can't I move here with you?"

"Mate, I'd want that more than anything in the world" I said "But you can't. I'm sorry. You have to stay at your mother's"

"It's not fair" he said angrily.

"No, it isn't, I know. I'm really sorry buddy. There's nothing I can do about it"

He came and sat next to me "I just don't want to be there dad. It's so bloody far away from anything. I hardly see my friends anymore because it's too difficult to get to them, and football is a nightmare. I'm constantly having to bum lifts because mum can never take me. She's always too busy"

I didn't know about that, and it made me sad. "If you're ever stuck for a ride, you let me know ok? I'll drop whatever 'm doing and come get you"

He hugged me and started crying. Fucking hell. I knew things were bad, but not this bad. This wasn't good. I felt helpless. I wanted to help him, make everything ok, but I just couldn't. What the fuck was going on that she couldn't take him to football? She knew it was his life. Would a chat with her help? *A fucking baseball bat would help!* Shhh. Grown-up talking.

"I'll have a chat with her and see what's going on. Would that help?"

"Not sure it would, it's not really mum, it's him. He keeps harping on about us being more independent and that we're spoiled"

Ok, now I'm angry.

I'll get the fucking bat...

I was silent for a moment, thinking about what to say.

James must have sensed my unease, because he said "I'm sorry, I didn't mean to mention him. I know its hard for you"

"It is mate. I don't like the idea of some other guy bringing up my kids"
"I don't like it any more than you do, if that makes any difference?" he said
I hugged him "Of course it does mate. I miss you so much"
Tears were coming. *Hold it together!*
I did. Just about.
"Dad?"
"Yes?"
"You know I can hear your inner voice right?"
"Yeah I know buddy. I'm working on it"
We both laughed. There was a little more chat about football, and I found out a bit more about his school life. He was still seeing his girlfriend, but the distance made it a bit harder. Apart from the mum situation, his life was exactly what I'd hoped it would be; normal. I was proud of this young man. He was getting on with his life, despite the hardships. I say hardships, I mean the shitty fallout from the divorce, moving away, etc. You get the picture.
"What's for dinner?" he asked after we'd finished chatting
"Dunno. Chrissy is making something, we'll see"
"I'm sure it'll be good then" he said
"I'm sure it will. And I'm sure I won't take that personally" I ruffled his hair. "I'll give you a shout when it's ready"
I got up and walked out.
"Dad?"
"Yep?"
"I love you"
"Love you too buddy"
My heart swelled. What a kid.

Elsie was sat on her bed listening to music.
Don't ask me what it was, it all sounds the bloody same to me.
"Hey Ello" I said and sat next to her.

"Hi daddy" she said and hugged into me "How you doing tiger?"
"I'm ok daddy. I miss you"
"I miss you too kiddo" I kissed her head "How's things at school?"

Cue a tirade of girly gossip that went on and on for almost ten minutes. I hardly got a word in edge ways. The occasional "Yep" or "Yes" was all I managed. She was doing just fine. She wasn't into sports, and spent most of her time gossiping with her mates on her phone or pad, or whatever.
It was all foreign to me, and I found it a bit weird, but I guess I'm of a generation where we actually spoke to people, and were outside all the time.
"How's things with your mum?" I asked.
She thought for a moment "Ok I think. Not for James though"
Jesus, how grown p was this kid? Wow. "I know, I've just been talking to him" I said. Again, I was proud of my child. She was less worried about herself, more about her brother.
"He's not happy. He misses his friends" she said "And I think he wants to live with you"
"I know tiger, I know. There's nothing I can do about it though. I need you to look out for him for me ok? If you see something about to happen, hug him and make it ok"
"I will daddy" We hugged, and she asked about my life. Wow. Ok. I told her all about Kyle, and how Steve was. She asked about her grandparents, and Chico of course. I promised we'd go see them in the morning.

Little tangent. Mini one?

I was taken aback at Elsie asking how I was.
I don't get that very often. From anyone.

I always make an effort to ask how people are, and rarely, if ever, get asked in return. It bugs me a bit, because sometimes I need an outlet too. Don't get me wrong, I never complain. I'm an excellent listener, and if I'm talking to you, you'll get 100% of my attention and eye contact. I just think people get so focused on downloading to me that they forget to ask. Ask me how I am sometimes ffs. I'm not always ok. People like me mask. It's all hidden. Drip over.

I went back down to the kitchen, where Chrissy was busy making dinner.
"You ok?" she asked when she saw me.
"Yeah, I think so" I said.
"You can cry if you need to" she said sincerely.
"No, I'll be ok" *No, you're not you prick…*
She could see that I wasn't, and came over "Come here" she said, holding out her arms.
I fell into them and started crying. "Shhhh, it's going to be ok" she said, stroking my head.
"I miss them so much" I said, sobbing.
I felt a pair of small arms hugging into me "It's going to be ok daddy" Elsie said.
Shit. This was a low moment. Caught out crying like a baby. Fuck. *Is it a low moment though?* What? *Why should you be ashamed to show your kids how much you miss them?* Good point.
I got myself together, wiped my eyes, and kissed both my beautiful ladies. "Thank you both"
"I'll do the table" Elsie said, and went off to do just that. Chrissy looked at me, and gestured for me to look behind me.
James was sat halfway down the stairs, tears in his eyes.
"Hey, buddy, come here" I said.
He came down, and hugged into me tightly "I'm so sorry dad" he sobbed. *Jesus, what the fuck was going on here? Like a fucking blub-fest.* Shut up you.

"Sorry for what mate?" I asked.
"I made you sad"
"Hey" I said, holding him at arm's length "You only make me happy, you hear? None of this is your fault, never think that"
"Would a Chrissy hug make it better?" his sister teased.
He went bright red "Shut up you!"
"Don't tease your brother" I said to Elsie.
"Hey, I'm always available for hugs" Chrissy said holding her arms out.
Awkwardly, James walked over and accepted the hug. Chrissy made a point of shaking him about a bit "Nothing like a good hug eh?" she laughed.
James still looked super embarrassed, but laughed too.
"Right" she said, letting him go "Dinner is ready, sit"
We all sat around the table and enjoyed a delicious meal, and happy chat. I loved these moments; it reminded me of how much I missed having a family around the table. It would be quite a few years before it would be the daily norm sadly.

We left the kids to clear up and do dishes, and went to sit in the living room. "You ok?" she asked.
"Yeah, I'm ok. More than ok" I said. Truth. I was. "You embarrassed the hell out of James" I joked.
She laughed "I know, he's a funny sausage" she winked.
"Poor lad still has a bit of a crush I think" I said
"Can you blame him?" she giggled "Look at me"
I threw a cushion at her "Modest as always"
"Hey." she said "Tidy remember?"
"Matter of opinion" I said. Shoulder punch. "Ouch!" Hadn't had one of those for a while.
"Deserved that" she said.
"Fair"

When the kids had finished and joined us, we sat and watched a movie. It took a while to decide, but we eventually ended up watching Aladdin. No complaints from anyone; it was a favourite. I loved Robin Williams as the Genie. Genius Genie.

The kids went to bed after the movie, and we were left on our own. I say gone to bed; they went off up to their rooms; James likely gaming, Elsie texting her mates. We didn't see them till morning. Modern life eh?
We went out to the bar and had a few drinks and listened to some great music. A perfect end to a perfect day.

In bed, I did my usual and reflected on the day before sleep. What a day it had been. I had been looking forward to seeing the kids. I had no idea the amount of emotion I had stored up, it all came flooding out.
In front of the kids. I hadn't intended for them to ever see me like that, but in the end I suppose it's good to see that it's ok to show your emotions. It was good for them to see the impact the divorce had had on me, and how much their not being here affected me.

Satisfied, and happy, I put my headphones in and hailed a Hansom to take me to Scotland Yard. Holmes and Watson were waiting for me. "Ah, Beckett, how jolly nice of you to join us" Holmes commented sarcastically…

Day 7, Saturday, 16th of June.

I woke the following morning completely refreshed. I had slept like a baby. Chrissy was already up, and I could smell pancakes in the air. I got up, had a very quick shower, dressed, and went downstairs.
"Wow, morning" I said. Everyone was already up, sat around the table, waiting for me to show up.
"Morning sleepyhead" Chrissy smiled.
"Daddy, Chrissy made pancakes!" Elsie beamed.
"Well, let's not get too excited" Elsie added quickly "I've never made them before, so they could be terrible"
"Look good to me" James said, and blushed immediately. "The pancakes" he added awkwardly .
"I think we got that" Elsie said, confused.
"Looking forward to this" I said, sitting down, breaking the tension.
"Tuck in" Chrissy said. And immediately, kid's hands shot out and helped themselves to the stack in the middle of the table.
I got one for myself, added some strawberry, banana, raspberries, drizzled some golden syrup over it, and got stuck in. "Mmmm" I said with a mouth full "Nice"
"Yes, they are, aren't they James" Elsie teased.
He looked awkward, I felt sorry for the lad.
"Stop teasing your brother. Leave the boy alone to eat"
There was no more teasing, only eating. Happiness.
Later, after breakfast, I was down in the utility room putting the kid's school uniforms in the machine, when Elsie came in, asking when we could go see Chico.
"Just let me chuck this in, and we'll get ready" I said.
She seemed unusually keen to get out, should I read more into this?

Maybe she just needs a bit of fun and comfort. You offer one, the dog offers both. Fuck you very much. *Just sayin…*

I set the machine to work, and went off to see if the rest of the clan were ready to go. Chrissy was sat in the living room, reading a book; Expert Witnessing in Forensic Accounting.

"Wow, bit of light reading?"

"Mmmm, it's superb. You want it after me?"

"Give it a miss thanks" I laughed. "You ready to head out? Elsie is desperate to see Chico"

"She ok? Seems a bit quiet. She's usually really bubbly, but seems subdued"

"Yeah, I thought that, no idea. She didn't say anything last night"

"Maybe seeing Chico and having a bit of fun will sort her out"

"You saying I'm not fun?" I asked.

"No, not at all, just… Well, you know…"

"Yes?" I pushed.

"It might be nice for us to get out and about a bit more"

"You think we don't get out enough?"

She took a breath. "Ok, here's what I'm trying to say; I think it's probably better to get out than for the kids to sit in their rooms"

"Hmmm" I said.

"Hmmm? Just hmmm?"

"Well, obviously I'm a bit hurt…"

"Sorry, I didn't mean it in a bad way. I thought maybe we could get a National Trust membership or something, get out and about a bit more"

"I like that idea" I did. It was something I'd never considered.

"There are loads of trust properties we can go to in the area. Just thought it would add a bit of variety"

"Ok, I'll sort it" I said with enthusiasm.

"No need" she said, pulling cards out of her purse "Done" She handed me my membership card.

"Of course it is…" I rolled my eyes. Cue a shoulder punch.

"Don't be a dick Beckett, I was being proactive"
I rubbed my shoulder "Hmmm, I appreciate it, I really do. One stipulation though"
"Ok…"
"If either or both of them don't want to go, we should not argue. We can always go ourselves. I don't want to make them feel like they have to if they genuinely don't want to"
"Why wouldn't they want to?"
"New generation Lenoir, everything is online. We're different, it's weird. I struggle with it, but have accepted that they are tied to devices"
She took a moment to consider. "Yeah, you're right. Kids are glued to screens these days. Ok, deal."
"Shake on it" I stuck out my hand.
She took it, but instead of shaking it, pulled me down on top of her. "Deal" she kissed me. Passionately.
"Guys? We're ready when you are" James said from the door.
In my haste to get up, I rolled off the sofa, and almost landed on the coffee table.
"Ouch. Shit! Erm, yeah ok mate, coming"
Laughter from both kids. And Chrissy. Elsie spoke up. "Daddy, it's ok, we've seen people kissing before you know?"
"I know sweetie, just… Well, nothing I guess." I was embarrassed for some reason.

Worth a tangent here. Even if it's just a small one.

Right. This might just be me, but I'll ask anyway. Were/are you weary about your kid(s) seeing you smooch with your new partner? I was a bit scared of them seeing it, because I was worried they wouldn't understand. Understand? Yeah, couple of things I guess.
1. We still think you and mum should be together; why are you kissing someone else?

2. They understand, but it's too soon.
3. They understand, but just don't want to see it
4. They don't understand; how can you have moved on so quickly?
5.

I'm sure there are variations I can't think of, so insert your own at 5…

5. You're just a dickhead? Everyone except you…

Irrational? Stupid? Sure. But I thought some of those. I was scared of how the kids would react. Justified? *Ancient?* (Bit of a KLF ref there...)
Call it what you like, it was a bit strange, and I was still uncomfortable with them seeing it. Obviously, this would go away, but never quite completely.
There is still a microscopic part of me that it worried. Yet another one of those mental issues we have to deal with after a divorce. Add it to the list!
Anyway, irrational thoughts over…
Thank fuck for that…

"She's right dad, it's really ok. We don't mind" James said, saving me.
I went over and took them into my arms "Thank you"
"Yeah, sure" James said "Can we go now?"
"Yeah, let's go" I said, eager to get away from the awkwardness.
We went off out into the world. It was pleasant out; sun was shining, not a cloud in sight.
We walked through the village, which was already bustling with life. Happy, smiling faces everywhere.
"Can we stop at the cafe?" Elsie asked.
"Erm, we can't. Uncle Steve is in London with Willow, visiting her mum"

"Oh" she said, with obvious disappointment.
"Sorry Ello"
"It's ok Daddy" she said, and ran off ahead with James to play pooh sticks on the bridge.
Was it ok though? I could see something else in her eyes; sadness. I looked at Chrissy, she had seen the same thing.
"Something isn't right" she said.
"I know. But not sure what it is."
"You want me to try talking to her?"
"Would you mind?" I asked. She'd probably do a better job than me.
"Of course not, that's what I'm here for, right?"
"Right" I smiled "Thank you"
Apparently, Elsie had won the pooh sticks race, and was busy gloating when we caught up to them.
"Yeah, yeah, I'll get you next time" James said.
"Come on you two, let's get going" I said, defusing the situation before it escalated.
They ran on ahead, and got to mum and dads before us.

Mum already had the kettle on when we walked in. The kids were out in the garden with dad and Chico. I hugged mum, who asked if I was ok. She still text me every day to ask, as she had every day since I told her about the "incident". "Yes, I'm fine mum" I reassured her.
"Good." she said, and went off to hug Chrissy saying "Pour the water into the teapot would you?" The kettle had just finished boiling, so I did as I was told. I smiled to myself.
This teapot. Wow. It must be ancient, I remember it being around when I was a child. *Yeah, that is ancient then!*
Fuck you. A creature of habit, mum still used the same teabags too, although they were pyramid shaped now.
I opened the biscuit tin; same old biscuits.

Not that I was complaining, I mean, who doesn't love choc digestives? I took one, and started getting the cups ready. Same old cups on the shelves, same old cutlery set in the draw. Their generation is much more frugal than ours I thought. They were raised in post-war Britain; the land of rationing. They valued their possessions far more, and weren't so quick to change what they had. If it worked; it worked. Why replace it?
I would occasionally change my crockery completely, especially if I spotted something I really liked. This was foreign to my parents. This probably also explained why they had a lot of money saved away, whereas I did not.
That's because the divorce cost a fucking fortune, the fucker took you for a ride. Yeah, still is costing a fortune too. Depressing. I shook my head to snap out of the thought process.
"You ok there?" Chrissy asked.
"Yeah, I'm fine" I smiled. She gave me that squinty eyed suspicious look, but didn't probe further.
"You want tea outside?" I said to mum?
"Yes, I think so" she said cheerfully
I put everything on a tray and started walking out ahead of them. "Get that would you?" I said to Chrissy, nodding at the biscuit tin.
"Some things never change" my mum laughed "He did always love a few biscuits with his tea.
"Noted" Chrissy said with a smile, and picked up the biscuit tin.

Out in the garden, dad and the kids were busy throwing a ball for Chico, who was in heaven, running around like a dog possessed. It was a happy scene, and I was happy to sit and observe. Elsie looked so happy.
Maybe that's what she's been missing.
What?
The dog.

You reckon?
Poss right?
Yeah, poss. I'll mention it to Chrissy.
"What?" Chrissy asked
"Erm, maybe it's the dog that she misses?" I offered, embarrassed at being caught out yet again.
Yet a-fucking-gain…
"Good point inner voice. I'll ask" she winked.
Hah! Vindication! Shut up…
I reached into the biccy tin and took 4 biscuits.
"Whoa!" Chrissy said.
"Hey, little and often right?" I smiled cockily.
"Little and often?" Mum asked. Ah, shit. Hadn't told mum…
"Yeah, I went to see the doc yesterday, and I have low blood pressure"
"Very low" Chrissy cut in.
"Yes, thank you, very low." I said.
"He's been fainting" Chrissy added.
"Yes, ok, thank you nurse Lenoir" I said, giving her a look.
"You've been fainting?" Mum asked, obviously concerned.
"Yes" I said, but added quickly "Not often though"
"How long for?" she asked, with a tinge of anger in her voice
"A few months or so" I said quietly.
"What? And you didn't tell me?" she said, trying to keep her voice down so the kids wouldn't hear.
"Well, you know, I didn't want you to worry" I said. It was all I could think of at the time.
"It's my job to worry about you Jack" she said "Are you on tablets?" She would never admit it, but she was angry. Disappointed even. I could tell, and felt like shit for it.
"No, I just have to monitor for now, go back in a few weeks" I said. "I have to eat little and often, and make sure I have salt in my diet"

In an effort to calm herself down, mum launched into an epic tale of family members and friends with low blood pressure. I was relieved, but likely not off the hook…

I made sure to say "Yes mum" at the right moments, to reassure her I was taking her advice and listening. Wow, nice. I gave Chrissy a look that said "Just you wait…"

My phone buzzing gave me the get out of jail free card I needed; it was Steve. "Got to take this" I said, and went inside.
"Hey man, all ok?"
"Yeah, sound. Just wanted to let you know we're driving back up this evening."
"That's good news mate. Willow all ok?"
"Yeah, she's right as rain, and desperate to get home. She loves her mum, but you know…"
"Yeah, I get it"
"She also wants to know if you want to pop round later?"
"You sure? I asked
"Yeah, like I said, she's perfectly fine. She's keen to get back to normal."
"I have the kids, that gonna be ok?"
"Fucking right it is, I miss my little cretins"
"Genius. What time you thinking?"
"About seven?"
"Sounds like a plan"
"Later fucknut"
"Later matey"

I dialed off, and went to tell Chrissy the good news. The kids would be happy, they were dying to see Steve. I was too.
The reaction was as expected; the kids were ecstatic. As was Chrissy of course, but not quite so outwardly enthusiastic.

After tea, we all went out and took the dog for a walk. A good walk is good for the soul, and this one was no exception.

It did wonders for my anxiety, and it looked like it was doing the same for Elsie. *You think she's anxious?* Maybe, maybe not. I was going to talk to Chrissy about it later, but I also made a mental note to mention it to Pam next time I saw her. She seemed ok during the walk, but I could see something in her eyes, something familiar, but out of reach for the moment. Rather than dwell on it, I put it on a shelf, and enjoyed the time with my family. Smiling faces, wagging tail, summer sun. Bliss.

When we got back home, I did lunch, and the scatter happened; James went off out to see his friends, and Elsie went up to her room to probably speak to her friends or watch something. Neither had a lot of homework, so it was all good with me. Chrissy went out to do a bit of gardening, leaving me on my own in the kitchen. What to do? I was at a loose end. I pottered around the house, tidying, bit of dusting. Then I got bored. Man, it was quiet. Too quiet. Dangerously quiet. This wasn't good for me. Come on Jack, do something. In the end, I went out and washed the car. Didn't really need it, but it was something to do. After that, I checked in on Elsie; she was sat with her headphones on, watching hair styling videos. I gave her a drink and a couple of biscuit, then left her to it. Chrissy was still out in the garden, so I made her a cup of tea.
"Oh, lifesaver" she said, wiping her brow.
"Looking good" I said.
"Me, or the garden?"
"Both" I said, and kissed her. The sweet smell of her perfume filled my senses; she smelled of absolute loveliness. Even when covered in dirt after working in the garden, she still managed to exude femininity. *Can I say it?* Go on then. *What a woman.*
"Thank you" she said, taking a sip of her tea. I was going to have a quick shower, then maybe take Ello out for an ice cream, what you think?"
"Sounds like a great idea, she'll like that"

"Great. Hey, erm, do you mind me calling her Ello? I mean is it weird?" she asked.
"Not at all, why?" I said.
"Dunno, just don't want to seem over familiar if that makes sense"
"I wouldn't worry; be as familiar as you like. The kids love you"
She smiled with obvious relief. Not sure why she needed me to verify that, she knew the kids liked her. *She's still finding her feet, testing boundaries*. True, true.
"Right" I said "If you guys are heading out, I'm going to go for a run"
"No fainting though ok. Take a measurement recently?"
"Yes thanks, been filling in the sheet religiously" I wasn't lying; I had been taking measurements regularly. I was as worried as her about my health, so was doing my best to follow doctors' orders.
"Good to hear. Still low?"
"Not as low as yesterday, but I guess, yeah"
"Make sure you eat when you get back, ok?"
"I will nurse"
"Nurse eh? Maybe I should get a uniform…" she said teasingly
"Get to the shower!" I commanded "Make it a cold one"
She giggled, and disappeared off into the house. I sat in the sun for a while, enjoying the warmth on my skin. I must have fallen asleep, because I was woken by Elsie telling me they were going out to get ice cream.
"Silly daddy. Don't fall asleep in the sun, it's not good for you" she giggled
"Away with you!" I jumped up and chased my giggling girl out of the front door.
I yawned, had a stretch, and went up to get changed.

Stretching and warming up on the drive, I noticed a removal truck had pulled up, and they were emptying the house next door.
I hadn't seen a for sale sign. What's going on? Weird. I finished my warm up and trotted off on my run. Ah, bliss. Whilst I loved running, as it gave me time to clear my mind, I was not a natural runner. As said before; I hit my stride after about 6k, but only run 5k's so it was a slog every time. I have never experienced the "runners' high". What the fuck even is that anyway?

Tangential quickie.

I have done some running in my life, trust me. I used to do 6-7 miles every day, and never experienced anything but misery. Runners' high? Pah! Some people are just lucky I guess.
Done.

Thinking of my low bp, I suddenly thought; what if 5k isn't enough? Should I run further?
Brain: Hmmm, that might be a good idea. Smiley face emoji.
Body: absolutely fucking not you prick. Angry face emoji.
Body wins. I stuck to my usual 5, and called it a day. Good run followed by a cool shower.

Still a bit hot, I sat out in the garden with a beer. Deserved. *Truth brother, cheers.* Alcohol free beer… *You're a melt…*
I had the doors of the bar open, and was listening to some Donny whilst enjoying the sunshine. Life was good wasn't it? Despite the fucking nightmare of the recent past, I had it good. Didn't I? *Sure do man. Could do with a shag though eh?* Drop it. Told you, wait till the holiday. *Oh I am, trust me.*
Quick watch check told me it was only just after half past three. Wow, time is crawling. Nice!

I took my t shirt off, lay back, and chilled.   (Donny = Donavon Frankenreiter btw…)
Don't know how much time had passed when a sudden shadow blocked out the sun.
I opened my eyes to see what it was.
"Hey, thought I'd join you"
It was Chrissy. In a fucking bikini, smokin! Truth.
"Hey, you're like a fucking ninja you know that?" I said.
"Funny. Thought I was a witch?" she said, leaning back in the chair next to me.
"That too" I laughed. "How'd it go?"
"Hmm, ok" she said, and took a swig of my beer "Ugh, warm"
I laughed "sorry, that's been there for a while"
"Yuck. Erm, yeah, it went ok I think. She was fine, but you can tell there's something going on. Don't know what it is though. I asked her if there was anything wrong, or anything she wanted to talk about, but she just said no. bit too quickly for my liking."
"She's definitely off. I might have a chat with her mother and see if she knows"
"Good idea, though girls tend not to tell their mum's very much."
"They don't?"
"Mommy's boys, Daddy's girls Jack"
"Really? That's a thing?"
"Sure it is. I was closer to my dad, never really confided in my mum"
"Wow. I thought I was close to both of them" I said.
"Different circumstances; the divorce has strengthened your bond with James. Plus, he hates living at his mums"
"True, that makes sense."
"Have a chat with your ex and see what's going on"
"I will. But right now, right here; I don't want to think about that woman"
I lay back in my seat and resumed my chill out.

Chrissy did the same. It was quiet, although I knew I had this gorgeous woman lying right next to me. *In a fucking bikini!* Yeah, you said that already. *Look at her!* I turned my head; she looked fantastic.

"Thanks, don't look too bad yourself" she said, her eyes still closed.

I remained silent, and faced front, embarrassed at my latest faux-pas.

In the background, the music changed to ALO, and I found myself drifting off. Again.

(ALO= Animal Liberation Orchestra, check them out)

When I opened my eyes, I found that:
a. I was no longer in the sun.
b. Chrissy had disappeared.

I stood, put my T back on, and went off to see where everyone was. Clock in the kitchen indicated 16.59. That explained both a. and b. above...

Elsie and Chrissy were busy getting dinner together. Looked like salad, which was perfect.

"Hey you two"

"Hey daddy" Elsie said, peeling boiled eggs "Nice sleep?"

"Yes thank you" I laughed.

"Good. Sleep is important" she said, placing a peeled egg in a bowl.

"Yes, it is" I said and kissed her head. "Dinner looks good"

"You know what time James is getting back?" Chrissy asked

"No idea" I picked up my phone and dialled his number. He answered after a few rings. After a brief conversation, I ascertained that he wouldn't be home for dinner as he was eating at his mates. He would be back in time to go to Steve's though.

"Just the three of us" I said, putting my phone down.

"Ok, no worries" she said, and set the table for three. "He'll be back to go to Steve's though?"

"Yeah, he's having dinner at his mate's"

"Lucky him" Elsie said with a distant look.

I went over, picked her up, and took her outside. I set her down in in a chair. "What's going on Ello?"

She looked at me like a lost sheep, and started crying.

I took her in my arms "Hey, what's up princess?"

Between sobs, she started telling me what was going on. It was all bad; she was being bullied at school. Fuck. Three girls were picking on her because her parents were divorced, telling her it was all her fault. They were pushing her about, and messing with her lunch. Fucking hell.

I was enraged. Nobody picks on my girl. Rather than showing it, I reassured her that it was nothing to do with her at all, and that she shouldn't listen to them. I would take her to school on Monday and sort it out.

We went back inside, and sat down to eat. Dinner was a bit subdued, despite my best efforts to lighten the mood. Ello disappeared off upstairs, leaving half her dinner.

"What's going on?" Chrissy asked with urgency.

"She's being bullied at school"

"Fucking hell. By who? I'll kill them"

"Three girls, basically picking on her because her parents are divorced. Apparently they're telling her it's her fault and pushing her around"

"Oh my god. Tell me who they are, I'll sort it" she said, enraged.

"Easy tiger, they're ten remember? I'll sort it Monday"

"What are you going to do?"

"I have an idea" I said.

"Care to expand?"

"Nope, but I'll sort it. Trust me"

"Ok. You'd better, or I will" she warned.

"Don't worry, I will."
"Should I go see if she's ok?" she asked.
"Nah, leave her for a bit. She needs some time to gather herself before we go the Steve's."
"Ok, if you're sure"
"I'm sure. Daddy's girls remember?"
She just rolled her eyes and started clearing the table. I helped out, and did the dishes.

James walked in at about half past six. I was sat playing a bit of guitar, and Chrissy was reading her epic book. We hadn't seen Elsie since she went up after dinner.
"Hey buddy" I said, putting the guitar down "Good day?"
"Brilliant day" he said, beaming. He hadn't seen much of his friends since the move, except in school of course.
"Glad to hear it" I said smiling. At least one of them was in a good place. *Though he wasn't was he?* Fuck. No, he wasn't. But he was happy in this moment, which is all that mattered. *Truth.*
"I got time for a quick shower?" he asked.
"Sure, go for it" I said, and he ran off upstairs.
"He sounds happy" Chrissy said from behind her book
"Yeah he does"
"That's good" she smiled, and put her book down. "I'll go freshen up before we go" she said, kissed me and went up to the bedroom. I had no idea what "Freshen up" meant, but I guess women have their little secret ways eh…
I took the quiet time to take another bp reading before we went; still too low. Sigh.
Oh well. I put the kit away and went to see if everyone was ready to go.
The kids were already milling about out on the drive.
"You ready?" I called up to Chrissy.
"Two secs" was the reply.

I went out and waited with the kids; they were kicking a ball about. Elsie looked happy. Looked. But now I knew she really wasn't. I really needed to speak to Helen, but it would have to wait till tomorrow now.
"Finally" I said as Chrissy appeared.
"Hey, can't rush perfection right" she said.
"True" I kissed her "You look wonderful"
"Smoothie" she smiled, and took my hand as we walked down to Steve's.

It was a pleasant enough walk across the village; the sun was out, there were lots of hanging baskets in full bloom, the streets were tidy, people were friendly. I love this place. Chico barked at the window as we walked past mum and dads, prompting giggles from Elsie.
We waved at dad, who came to see what the dog was barking at. The kids ran up ahead and were banging on the front door when we got there.
"Ok, ok, ok! Oi! What are you horrible cretins doing, banging at my door?" Steve yelled through the open window.
The door opened "Hey, give the door a rest would ya?" Then; big smile "Come here you two" he took the kids in his arms "Oh, I've missed you guys"
"We miss you too Uncle Steve" Elsie said, hugging into him.
"Come on, I've got a selection of ice creams in the freezer for you to devour" he took two happy kids inside. We followed them inside, where we found Willow in the kitchen making snacks.
"Hey you" Chrissy said, and the ladies hugged
"Hey, how are you guys?" Willow asked, as I took my turn for a hug.
"Us? Never mind about us" Chrissy said "How are you?"
"Ach, I'm fine, really. Nothing wrong at all" she said dismissively.

"You sure?" Chrissy persisted, now placing her hand on Willows little bump.
She placed her hand over hers "I'm sure"
"Aye-aye!" I said, pointing at her hand "The fuck's going on here?"
"Oh this?" she held out her hand, with engagement ring on her finger.
"Oh my god!" Chrissy clapped excitedly "Really???"
"Yeah, isn't it beautiful? He proposed last night. He said he was planning something super romantic, but it just seemed the right time"
"Oh wow, congrats" Chrissy said and they hugged again.
"Congratulations I said, smiling, kissing her cheek. I was happy for her, but obviously didn't have the same levels of excitement as Chrissy was showing.
Women always do better with these things. I went outside, where Steve was busy chatting to the kids. "Hey man"
"I'm gonna do boring chat with your dad now ok guys?" he said, and the kids wandered off into the garden with their ice creams.
"Boring chat?"
"Well, you know" he said, and hugged me "Good to see you buddy. You been ok?"
"I'm fine mate. Was more worried about you. And I see you popped the question"
"Well, it just seemed like the right time, you know? She was down, and overwhelmed, so I thought it might help her."
"You did good"
"I did?"
"You did"
"Thanks man that means a lot. Beer?"
"Of course"
We joined the ladies in the kitchen, and Steve passed around beer. Proper for us, alcohol free for Willow.

"To the happy couple" I said, and we clinked our bottles together.
"Thanks guys" Steve said.
"I love the ring, good choice Stephen" Chrissy joked.
"Well, you know, I have exquisite taste" he winked.
"I knew you had something to do with it" Willow exclaimed, pointing at Chrissy "This lump would never have chosen this by himself"
"Hey, seriously?" Steve said, hurt.
"To be honest, he had three, and this was one of them, so technically he did choose it" Chrissy added in his defence.
"Thank you" Steve said gratefully "I'm not totally useless"
"Not totally… I said.
"Oh, I see how it is eh. Pick on poor old Steve. Nice"
We all laughed. Chrissy and Willow sat at the table talking about the engagement, and wedding plans. Bit early, I thought, but that's women for you. I walked over to the patio door with Steve to watch the kids.
"So" Steve said quietly "When are you going to propose to her?"
I almost spat out my beer "What?" *What the fuck??*
"Don't be a bell end Beckett, you know what I mean. Bag her, before she fucks off and finds someone more interesting"
"Fuck you" I said "More interesting? Jesus, cheers mate" *He's got a point…* And you can fuck off and all!
"Seriously though" Steve said "You planning on marrying her?"
"Hadn't even thought about it mate, bit soon, you know?"
"Ah, of course, sorry. Well, you can always get engaged, and marry in a few years"
"Hmmm, yeah I guess so"
"Think about it. How's this doing?" he said, putting his hand on my head.
"All good at the moment. Saw the doc yesterday, I have low blood pressure, hence the fainting"

"Wow, really? Seems weird. You're pretty fit and healthy"
"Yeah, go figure, right?"
"Things with the other one going ok?" Helen…
"Think so, we don't really talk. No need to I suppose"
"Good. And those two" he nodded towards the kids in the garden.
"Hmmm. Different story mate. James hates living at his mums, it's getting worse."
"Difficult one, not like you can just tell her to fuck off and have him living with you"
"No, wish I could"
"Ello?"
"Wow, yeah, Ello." I took a breath "She's being bullied at school"
"Who the fuck is bullying my girl?" he pounded his fist on the table "I'll fucking beat the shit out of them"
"Yeah, my reaction too mate, trust me. Some girls are picking on her, telling her the divorce was her fault etc. They're pushing her around and messing with her lunch"
"Fucking hell, I'll kill the little fuckers. Who?"
"Easy man, I'll sort it on Monday"
"You'd better, or I will"
I laughed.
"What the fuck is so funny?" he said angrily.
"No, no, just that Chrissy said exactly the same thing"
"Good girl. We can tag team the little bastards"
"Chill dude, I'm as angry as you are, but beating up nine year olds isn't going to help. Trust me, I'll sort it"
He was quiet for a moment, then said "Ok, make sure you do though"
"Promise"
Is it just me, or is he welling up? You're right, he is welling up.
"Hey, dude, it's going to be ok" I said, re-assuring him.
"I know, just makes me sad, you know? Poor little thing"

"I hear you mate"
We sat in silence for a bit, just watching Elsie run around the garden.
"You boys ok?" Chrissy asked, walking over
"Yeah, all good" I said.
"Cool, you wanna help set the table?"
"Sure"
"Out here" Steve said, sliding open the patio door.
We started ferrying out the bowls of finger foods to the garden table, it all looked very tasty.
The rest of the evening was spent around the table, picking at the delicious foods, and having a good laugh. It was good for the soul, and I could see how happy Elsie was on Steve's lap. He was holding on to her like a protective father. I loved him all the more for it.

Later, after the kids had gone to bed, I was sat in the bar with Chrissy enjoying a pint of Stout. We were talking about the evening, and about Elsie. I didn't really want to talk about it too much, and I think she got the message, as she soon changed the subject. It was her turn to be in charge of the music, and we had a variety of tunes from the 70s, 80s, and 90s. It was a pleasant end to a great day.

As always, I lay in bed, and went over the day's events. What was I going to do on Monday? *Yeah, what the fuck is your plan anyway?* No idea. I guess the school has its own procedures to follow if bullying is reported. I'd have to talk to them first, then just go from there. For now, I need to put it out of my mind, or I'll never sleep. Instead, I thought about what Steve had said about getting engaged. He had a point. I'll have a bit of a look at rings tomorrow. *Whoa! Steady on!*
Happy with that thought, I got my headphones and walked the foggy streets of Victorian London with Holmes.

Day 8, Sunday, 17th of June.

Sunshine.
What?
Sunshine.
What?
That feeling of euphoria? The sun is shining on your face.
I opened my eyes;
I looked around, Chrissy was already up, the curtains were open, and the sun was indeed shining in my face. Shit, you're right. *Of course I am.*
Wait, sunshine, open curtains? What fucking time was it? In a mild panic, I checked my watch; 08.23. With a sigh of relief, I fell back onto my pillow. It wasn't as late as I thought. Here's me thinking I've missed most of the morning, and it was still early. The smell of coffee caught my attention. On the bedside table was a steaming mug of java. What a woman.
I sat up, and sipped my coffee. Downstairs I could hear muffled happiness. I guessed Chrissy had made the kids breakfast. I vaguely smelled toast and eggs. Scrambled eggs. Stomach: Hey, get your lazy arse out of bed and fill me up. Yes sir. I obeyed. Took my coffee and went to find sustenance.
"Morning gang" I said, smiling as I walked into the kitchen. There they all were sat eating breakfast with happy faces. What a thing to wake up to.
"Morning daddy" Elsie said, James echoed her statement, but with a mouth full of food.
Chrissy got up and gave me a hug "Morning sleepyhead, you ok? Hungry?" Yes, we are!
"Moring, I'm ok thanks, food sounds great"
"Cool, you sit, I'll make you some"

I sat and asked how the kids were. They were both fine. What are we doing today? Hmm, I had to think for a bit.
"How about a beach day?" Chrissy said from the stove "It's going to be a lovely day"
Everyone was happy, so beach day it is. We ate breakfast, and the kids ran off to get ready. "No rush!" I shouted after them "I've got to pack the car yet"
"Beach day eh?" I said after they'd disappeared.
"Not good?" she asked, quizzically
"No, all good. Just a lot of stuff to find and throw in the car" I was thinking like an idiot, and I knew it. *Beat me to it dickhead. Think bikini...*
I held my hands up "Sorry. It's a great idea. I'm overthinking"
"You're entitled to think how you like" she said with a smile "But we're still going"
"I'll need some time to find all the kit in the garage"
"No problem right? I've got to shower and dress yet" she said, indicating that she was still in her pj's.
"Ok, you go do that, and I'll pack up the car"
"Deal" Somehow, I thought, you got the better end of the deal. Although, she'd have to drive, so even-Stevens.
To be fair, finding the stuff in the garage wasn't hard at all; it was all in one place. I brushed off the cobwebs and put it all in the boot. By the time I'd finished, the rest of the gang had assembled in the hall. "Oh, ok, all ready are we? Don't mind me. I'll need a few minutes to get ready after packing the car on my own" I said sarcastically.
Chrissy rolled her eyes "We'll wait in the car superhero"
Minutes later, we were on the road. Sun blazing, kids happily chatting away in the back. I looked over at Chrissy, she looked stunning. How the fuck does she manage to look so good all the time? No bikini though, sorry. *What? Fuck sake.* Swimsuit today. *Just as good.* Man, you're such a perv.
"Who's a perv?" Chrissy asked.

"What?"

"Oh, let me guess… Hey, inner voice, no bikini today sorry" she said laughing.

"Funny" I said. She was right though.

Thankfully, this part of the country is blessed with a lot of long, sandy beaches, so they're never massively overcrowded.

We pulled into the car park, and it was only half full. Genius. We managed to park close to the beach path, and the kids jumped out immediately. They had disappeared off down the path before I'd even gotten out of the car to go pay for the parking.

"Wow" Chrissy said laughing "They seem happy"

"They love the beach" I said proudly, and started loading myself up like a pack mule with the gear we'd brought. I followed Chrissy, who was carrying the kids' bags. We found a lovely spot in the sun, close to the water. I dropped all the kit I was carrying and looked around. "Wow, beautiful day eh?"

"Yeah, it is. Come on, let's get this done so we can relax"

We set up the wind breaker and the rest of our base-camp.

Five minutes later, we were running off into the water.

Fucking hell! We're outta here! The "lads" retracted into my body, desperate to find warmth. The water was cold, as it always was in the North Sea, but after a few minutes, you got used to it. *Not us! We're staying up here where it's warm!*

"Bit cold eh?" I said to Chrissy. She automatically lifted her arms to cover her chest.

"That's not what I meant" I said. My turn to roll my eyes.

"Well, you never know" she winked and lowered her arms.

Fuck yeah! It IS cold!

Shoulder punch.

"Ouch. I need to watch what I'm saying"

"Yeah you do you freak" she joked.

We sat floating in the water, watching the kids playing football on the beach.

"She looks happy today" Chrissy said.
"Yeah, she seems ok. Worried about tomorrow though"
"I'm going to come with you" she said. No room for argument.
"Ok. You know Helen might turn up right?"
"I can handle your ex" she winked.
"I'm more worried about her dealing with you" I laughed.
I kissed her "I love you Christelle Lenoir"
"I love you too Jack Beckett"
This would have been a perfect proposal moment. Good reminder. I need to start looking for a ring. I need ideas though. *Talk to Willow.* Another good idea. *Full of them me.* Full of something for sure…
Ok, drop the thought for now before you say something stupid. Roger that.
"Ok, I'm getting out" I said "The lads are complaining that it's too cold"
"Eh?" she said, then cottoned-on "Ah, I see. Who'd be a man eh?"
"Let's go see if we can find somewhere to get a hot drink" I said and walked out of the water. Holy fuck! It felt cold in the wind. Shitty fuck balls. I ran up to the camp and wrapped myself in a towel.
Chrissy walked up laughing "You're a wuss"
"Yeah, maybe, but I don't care"
I dried off and put a t shirt on.
"You ready now princess?"
"Funny. Let's go" I said.
I walked over to the kids, who were busy building a huge sand castle. James had dug out half the moat. It looked impressive.
"Wow, awesome work guys. We're off to get a cup of tea. James, keep an eagle eye on your sister. We'll be back soon"
"I'm not a baby daddy" Elsie protested.
"Yeah Jack, she's not a baby. Stay safe guys, won't be long" Chrissy said and dragged me away.

"Thanks for saving me"
"No problem" she laughed.
We walked hand in hand at the water's edge towards the cafe, which was about 500m up the beach.
"This is heavenly" she said, breaking the silence. "Promise me it will always be this way?"
"I promise" I couldn't promise of course, but she knew that. I also wished it could be like this forever. Perfection in life.
Another perfect time to propose... Shhh!

We sat and enjoyed a hot tea with a slice of banana loaf at the cafe, then got the kids ice creams before we walked back. The sand castle was almost finished when we got there. Elsie was just busy decorating it with stones, shells, and bits of driftwood she'd collected on the beach. James was about a foot away from the water with his ditch, meaning we made it in time to see the flooding of the moat. He stood proudly as the water slowly filled the moat. "Nice job son" I said, handing him his ice cream "Thanks dad" he said with a broad smile on his face. I turned to Elsie "And same goes for you madam" I said "Perfect job, it looks beautiful" She smiled proudly "It's a princess castle" James shook his head in frustration. I'm sure he wanted it to be some knight's stronghold or something. Princess castle was furthest from his mind. As usual though, he humoured his little sister. "It's pretty" he said. We all sat in the sand, admiring the splendour of the princess castle. The sun was shining, the water was calm, and the company was perfect. I sighed deeply.
"You ok?" Chrissy asked.
"Yeah, just thinking how perfect this is"
She nodded in agreement. No words were necessary.
"Hey, you two, time for a sun cream refresh" I said.
"Dad! I'm not a child" James protested.
I just gave him a look. He hung his head, and took Elsie over to camp and re-applied sun cream for both of them.

"Come on" I said jumping up "Football"
Chrissy jumped up, and booted the ball way down the beach.
"Oh yeah, I see how it is" I said, and ran off to retrieve the ball.

The rest of the afternoon passed all too quickly, and it was soon time to pack up and go back home. The sun had traversed the sky, and the tide had gone way out.
Reluctantly, we all packed up and made our way back to the car.
"Who fancies chips at the cafe?" I said after we'd finished packing the car.
"Me!" Elsie shouted.
"Ok, come on then" I took her little hand and we all walked down to the cafe to have our dinner on the beach. How long would it be before she didn't want to hold my hand anymore? Depressing thought. I shrugged off the sadness, and concentrated on the here and now. We ate our sausage and chips as the sun started sinking away in the sky. I'll say it again; perfection in life.

Obviously, when you do things like that, the point comes when it's just too chilly. That moment came a few minutes after we'd finished eating. "Daddy I'm cold, can we go now please?" Elsie said, rubbing her arms.
"Of course sweetness"
And with that, the magical afternoon was over. We headed back to the car, and the drive home. Ello soon fell asleep in the back, and James was content to sit with his headphones on, listening to god alone knows what.
Chrissy put her hand on my knee. "Today was great wasn't it?"
"Yes, it was" I agreed. I knew she was desperate for us to bond as a family unit. Not sure why she worried about it, the kids had accepted her completely. We *were* a family unit.
I put my head back, and stared out at the world flashing by.

"Hey, no sleeping Beckett, you've got to keep me awake" Chrissy warned.
She was right. I had to stay awake. Although my eyelids were saying otherwise… I shook myself awake.
"Yeah, I know, sorry"
"Talk to me about the holiday, you think we need to go shopping before we go?"
"Another day following you around the city? Erm…"
She giggled "Don't worry, I'm going into town with Willow on Saturday, you're off the hook"
I was glad to hear it. Schlepping around town all day was not my idea of fun…
We chatted a bit more about the trip, train versus driving to airport, etc, etc…
Soon enough, we pulled into the drive. I had a look around; we all looked knackered. I wasn't at all surprised when both kids disappeared straight up to bed. I was pooped too, and was guessing Chrissy was too. I decided to leave the stuff in the car till some other time. I just retrieved the wet towels and threw them in the washing machine.
It was only half past eight, too early for bed. Wasn't it? Chrissy yawned. "I'm off for a quick shower, I need to wash my hair"
"Ok, I'm just going to sit outside for a bit"
"Don't fall asleep" she winked, and wandered off upstairs, yawning as she went.
Contagious. I yawned deeply, got myself a bottle of water from the fridge, and plonked down on a seat in the garden. Wow, I was tired. Not just from exertion, but mentally tired. Double tired.

I woke with a shock. Fuck! Cold water was running down my legs. I'd fallen asleep and dropped my bottle of water. Laughter from beside me, told me that Chrissy had finished her shower and had joined me outside.

"Come on sleepyhead, let's go to bed" she said, holding out her hand.
I took it, and we went off to bed.

Needless to say, headphones weren't required. Nor did I have time to go over the day's events. I went out like a light.
Zzzzzz….

Day 9, Monday, 18th of June.

D Day. I woke up with a mixture of feelings; anger, determination, anxiety, fear.
Ugh, come on Jack, man up. Why are you scared? Of the school?
No, of course not.
Helen?
Not really, maybe just the combination of Chrissy and Helen together.
Fireworks.
Let's hope not.
Could be interesting…
Forget about it.
I looked over, and Chrissy was still asleep. Should I wake her? I looked at the time; no. Leave her be.
Quietly, I got out and went down to sort the kids' lunches. I got a bit of a shock when I found Elsie already up and dressed at the kitchen table.
"Morning daddy" she whispered.
"Morning sweat heart" I said "What are you doing up this early?" I knew the answer of course…
"I couldn't sleep" She looked both broken and all grown up at once. You wouldn't think that she was only 9. There was a feeling of utter sorrow and helplessness deep inside me. The thought of someone harming Elsie brought to bear all the parental instincts of wanting to protect my little girl from harm.

Too early for a tangent?

Have you been faced with a situation like this? Or maybe something else that threatened your child's well being?

I think my initial reaction was typical; I wanted to kill the little bastards. I won't talk about the resolution, because it would spoil the rest of the chapter, I just wanted to focus on the emotion/reaction. My instant reaction was to kill two kids. A couple of nine year olds. Wow.
I've read/heard something somewhere once: It's amazing how quickly the desire/need/want* to kill someone enters the human brain. (For *, enter whatever word you want)
It's true, right? If not kill, then beat the absolute shit out of as a minimum. NOBODY harms my child. NOBODY. Rant over.

She looked so fragile, I just wanted to make it all better. As mentioned in the tangent above, my initial reaction was to want to kill them. Realism kicked in pretty soon though thankfully, and I now knew I needed to follow the correct route; talk to the school. I couldn't help but wonder if she'd shown similar behaviours at her mother's, and why the fuck Helen hadn't noticed. How could she possibly not? What the fucking hell is wrong with her? My anger was now projecting in multiple directions. I know what you're thinking: *but surely she knows as you're meeting her at the school this morning?* Yeah, I was, but she seemed confused and angry when I had told her, and said she had no idea. How the fuck could she have no idea? I had almost lost my shit with her, but Chrissy had calmed me down. This was one of those occasions where I could come out of this better than her. I could score a point, have one over on her, etc. I know, I shouldn't think like that, but it's hard not to sometimes. I liked the idea of her owing me one.

"I'm sorry Ello" I said, and kissed her head "I can imagine, and all I can say is that I'm going to try make this better. Sadly, I can't just go out and kill them"
This made her giggle, and for a brief second, she looked like the old Elsie. For a brief second.

Then it was gone; replaced by the misery mask.
"I'll sort it, I promise"
"Thank you daddy, I know you will" she hugged me tight. I could feel all her fears, anxieties, and desperations in the hug; it almost made me cry.
"You want some breakfast?" I asked, trying to distract her
"Yes please daddy" she smiled.
"I'll make you some scrambled eggs" I winked. I wasn't going to tell her that her mother would be at the school, as I didn't want to upset her. She obviously hadn't mentioned it to Helen, and I'm guessing she was scared of her mum's reaction. I'd have a word with Helen, make sure she handled it properly.
Meanwhile, the smell of eggs and toast had obviously reached James' nose, and his brain had told him to investigate. He appeared, as if by magic, at the bottom of the stairs as I placed the plate on the table.
"Something smells good" he said, and sat.
I rolled my eyes and returned to the stove to duplicate my efforts. To his credit, he had gotten glasses of milk for him and his sister by the time I'd finished his breakfast. Well done.
I left the pair of them to it, and made a coffee to take up for Chrissy. She was already awake when I walked into the bedroom.
"Something smells good" she smiled "Scrambled eggs?"
"Yeah, the kids are already up and eating" I replied, handing her the mug.
"Wow, early" she took the mug and sipped "Ah, nice. Cheers"
"Yeah, Elsie didn't sleep, she's a bag of nerves"
"Poor girl, I just want to make it better"
"Yeah, me too. We're meeting Helen at half past nine in reception. That way Ello won't see her and get more upset"
"Good plan"
"You think the school will deal with it?" I asked.

"I hope so, I'll bloody make sure they do. They must have procedures in place to deal with situations like this"

"You'd think so eh. Do me one favour though?"

"Hmmm?" she said, mouth full of coffee.

"Please don't go bat-shit crazy on them, or try turn it into a demonstration to Helen of how much you care for Ello"

"What?" she said, clearly hurt.

"No, not in a bad way, and I'm sure you wouldn't anyway. Och, fucking hell, I'm messing this up"

"Yes you are" stern words…

"I'm not worried about dealing with the school, I'm worried about you and Helen. Together"

"I'm not going to act like a dick Jack"

"Man, this isn't going well. Can you see what I mean?" I said pleadingly, almost begging.

She put her mug down, and kissed me "I do, dumbass. Don't worry about me, I'll be on my best behaviour"

"Thank fuck for that" I said, relieved.

"What?" her head snapped around, fist poised.

"As in you understand. Not as in you'll be on your best"

"Ah, gotcha. You're lucky" she said, and lowered her punishment arm. "I'm going for a shower, you can make me breakfast"

I didn't even question it, I just got up and went to do as I was told.

In the meantime, the kids had vanished from the kitchen. Miraculously, however, they had cleared up and done the dishes. Sporadic giggles from the living room told me Ello was in there watching telly. James was up in his room packing his stuff, and would likely be waiting for the bathroom to be free. He didn't have long to wait, Chrissy was done. "Bathroom's free!" she shouted as she went into the bedroom. That was my cue to get my skates on and do breakfast.

Just under an hour later, I was parking the car by the school. I knew from experience not to even attempt to park at the actual school, so we parked a few roads away and walked the rest.
James deserted us before we got to the school gates; he'd spotted a group of mates. As he said bye, he whispered "Give them hell dad, before I get into trouble". The message was clear; sort it, or I will. I assured him I would. I couldn't be more proud of him. As expected, I saw parents I was friendly with, but got completely blanked by all of them. Charming, thanks.
Elsie seemed a bit embarrassed that her dad dropped her to the door; I assume her mother no longer did that. Sorry Ello…
"Ok, you ready?" I said to Chrissy.
"Yep, let's do this"
We walked around to the other side of the building to the reception entrance. Helen was already standing at the door, busy on her phone.
"Morning" I said as we approached. She hurried her phone away.
"Morning" she looked from me to Chrissy, and back to me with a thinly veiled look of anger that basically said "What the fuck is SHE doing here?"
"I didn't realise there would be three of us" she said angrily. Although I'd gone through this scenario in my mind several times already, and knew exactly how I would respond, I completely lost the ability to speak. Chrissy jumped in to cover.
"Well, it was either I come to this, or beat the shit out of a couple of nine year olds" she said.
I looked at Helen, expecting the worst. Wait, was that a flash of a smile??? *What the fuck?*
Instead of some shitty sniping remark, she simply said "Well, we can't have that now can we?" and walked in.
"No, I guess not" I said, looking at Chrissy, who mouthed "What the fuck?"

We followed her in, and signed in at reception.
The receptionist informed us that the head teacher would be right down, and we could take a seat if we wished.
Head teacher? Headmaster surely? What's happened to this world???
There was no time to sit; the headmaster walked in seconds later. He shook my hand "Jack, good to see you. Sadly not under the best of circumstances" He turned to Chrissy, and I made the introduction. "Nice to meet you Miss Lenoir" he smiled. "Ah, Mrs Beckett" he said, extending his hand to Helen. I cringed.
"Actually, it's Miss Stevens now" she corrected him, and shook his hand.
"Of course, of course. My apologies. Please, follow me to my office" he said, and led the way. I knew Mr Jackson well; I had attended this school. Helen had not. Advantage Beckett. *Not a game you penis.*
"Please sit" he said, showing us into his office. We drew up chairs to the desk, and sat.
"Now then" he continued, closing the door "Nasty business Jack, and I'm glad you came to me first. We don't get many instances of bullying, only three in all my years here, so I was extremely distressed to hear about it. Not as distressed as you all I imagine. I want you to know that I will deal with this immediately, the wheels have already been set in motion in fact"
"Oh?" Helen asked.
"I emailed the parents of the girls concerned on Friday, to inform them that they have been suspended pending investigation"
"That's good to hear" Chrissy said.
"It's a start" Helen said, less convinced "What further action will be taken?"
"Well, Miss Stevens" he started, but Helen cut in
"You can call me Helen"

"Well, Helen, we need to investigate as per standard school procedures, and will determine ultimate action upon completion thereof"
"Ultimate action?" I asked.
"Yes, yes. I must tell you that I have a zero tolerance of bullying in my school, as you know Jack, and previous instances resulted in expulsion."
"I like the sound of that" Elsie said, making Mr Jackson smile.
"I take no pleasure in doing so, but like I said, zero tolerance" he said.
"Will it be on their record going forward?" Helen asked.
He nodded "Indeed. Whichever school they go to from here will have full knowledge of the reasoning"
She seemed happy with the answer, but simply nodded in agreement.
"We do offer our students counseling, and can arrange that for Elsie with your permission? Miss Harding is our in-house counselor, and is very experienced. She also doubles as our drama teacher, and is extremely well liked by the children"
"I think that's a great idea" I said, both Chrissy and Helen adding their approvals.
"Excellent, I will arrange that this morning. You will hear the outcome of the investigation by the end of the week" he said, standing, thus nicely indicating the end of the meeting. "You have my word"
"Thank you Mr Jackson" I said, shaking his hand.
"Anytime Jack, and please, pass on my regards to the Fletcher boy. Remind him he still owes me for the window he broke in year 2" he smiled.
"Oh, I will" I laughed.
"Miss Stevens, Miss Lenoir" he said, shaking their hand in turn.

As we signed out of the school, Helen asked if I had a few minutes to talk sometime today.

I looked at Chrissy who said "Don't look at me, I don't mind"
Did I spy another suppressed smile from Helen??
"Erm, yeah, ok, how about two ish?" I said, still unsure.
"Yes, that works. I'll meet you in Steve's new place? Would like to see it"
"Yeah, ok, sure. See you there"
"Perfect" With that, she turned and left.
We stood in silence for a moment, watching her go, then Chrissy turned to me and said "What the fuck just happened?"
"I have no idea" I replied, dumbfounded.
"Did she just fucking smile at me?"
"Twice" I said.
"Twice?"
"Yeah, she did it earlier when she asked why you were here"
"She did? I must have missed that"
"I think she likes you" I laughed.
"What? Don't be stupid"
"Seriously. I think she likes you"
"Well, I couldn't care less. I don't like her. No offence"
"Zero taken. Come on" We walked back to the car and drove home.

Tangent (follow on)

So, I said in the tangent earlier that I didn't want to go too far into the resolution of the bullying affair, but let's look at it now. What do you think? What were you expecting? Originally, I had some grand gesture in mind where Jack made some emotional speech in the playground for all to hear. Then I thought about it. Whilst that would make good reading, it wouldn't be realistic. It's not in Jack's character.
Chrissy maybe, but not Jack. This school has a great way to deal with bullying, I admire them, and that's how it should be in every school.

However, being a parent governor myself, I know it doesn't really happen like that. But, my book, my reality. Would you have done it differently to Jack?

After we got home, Chrissy went up to the office as she had minutes before a meeting started.
We said a hasty goodbye, and I went off to my office. The walk did me good; I got to clear my head before getting down to business. I set an alarm on my phone so I wouldn't miss my appointment with Helen, and text Steve to give him a head's up. Within seconds of receiving the text, he called.
"What the fuck?"
"I know mate"
"Why here for fuck sake? Go somewhere else"
"Not my idea"
"I don't want her here"
"Not my idea"
"You're a prick"
"Bye"
I dialed off, smiling to myself, and went inside.

"Morning Kyle" I said "Sorry I'm late"
"No worries Jack, did you get it sorted?"
"Yeah, think so. We spoke to the headmaster, and I think it's all going to be ok"
"That's good news. Speaking from experience, there's nothing worse than being bullied at school"
"I'm sorry that happened to you mate"
"Yeah, me too. Perfect target though right?"
"Hmmm, not good though mate. No such thing as a perfect target. Kids can be cruel"
"Yes, they can" he said, obviously reliving the pain.
"Anyways mate, how are we for work this week?" I said quickly, changing the subject.

He brightened up straight away "Pretty good, enough to keep us busy all week"

"Great" I said, rubbing my hands "Let's get stuck in"

Ok Jack, let's get to work. I opened a video, and scanned through the rough footage.

Liked it immediately; it was all about Jazzmasters, my favourite guitar.

It was an absolute dream video to work on, I was loving every second. After what seemed like only ten minutes, my phone alarm buzzed; it was time to head to the café. Fuck sake. I'd been at it for almost 2 and a half hours.

Hey Jacko, you ready for this? No, I'm not. *Ach, come on, it'll be ok.* Could do without it.

"Hey Kyle, I got to go meet my ex-wife for lunch to talk about this morning, you want me to bring you anything?"

"Wow, really? Have fun with that. Erm, no thanks, I have lunch. I'm going to go sit on the bridge in the sun and eat."

"Wish I could join you" I said sadly "Oh well, see you in a bit"

"Good luck"

I rolled my eyes "Thanks"

I don't want to fucking do this. *Why not?* Why the fuck would I? Ugh. I was feeling nervous as hell. Don't know why. I didn't like being around her anymore, it wasn't good for me. *Suck it up man.*

I got to the café at ten to one, and there was no sign of her yet. Thank fuck.

Tinkle.

"Motherfucker"

"Hi Steve"

"You absolute fucking knosher, what the fuck were you thinking?"

"Dude. Not my idea, I told you"

"Fuck that, you could have suggested somewhere else"

"You know her right? You think she would have listened?"

"No, but you're still a fucking prick. Aaaargh! What a fucking nightmare"

"Chill out man, it'll be fine"

"Oh I'm sure it fucking will dickhead, I just don't want her here"

"I know mate, I do"

"Fuck off. I suppose you'll be wanting to eat and all?"

"Erm, yeah?"

"Fucking nora. I've got to feed her too?"

"Hey, what were you expecting at lunch time?"

"You're lucky it's quiet" he said, then looked over to the two ladies sat giggling at a window table. There was nobody else around "Pardon my French ladies, this fucknut has pissed me off is all"

"My apologies Ladies, didn't mean to disturb your lunch" I added.

"It's ok" one of them said, and waved a dismissive hand.

"We're enjoying ourselves aren't we Edith?"

Her friend agreed. "Well, in that case, I hope you enjoy the rest of your lunch, and the rest of the show" I winked.

"Never mind that you bell-end, what the fuck you want to eat?" Steve said, as the door opened.

"Steve, charming as ever" Helen said with a smile.

"Helen" he said, and lowered his head.

"Hi, how are you?" she walked over to the counter, obviously wanting to engage with him. Steve wasn't playing though.

"Ok ta"

I went to the rescue. "Hi, let's go sit outside" I said, trying to encourage her away from him.

She turned, and had a look around "I love the new café" she said "It's lovely, and you have an outside area too? Wow"

Steve remained silent.

She turned back to him, determined to get him to speak. Was she just stupid? Can I get a cappuccino please? Medium? Jack?" she turned to me.

"Oh, erm latte, large." Steve shot me a look, I shrugged.

"Ok" he said, and started making the drinks.

"I understand why you don't want to talk to me Steve, and I'm sorry" she said "But you can't hold it against me forever surely?"

"Oh, I think I can" he said without looking up.

"Ah. Ok. I see. Well, in that case, I'll just go sit outside" she said, crestfallen, and unsure of what to do with herself. She walked out to the garden, leaving me behind.

"Eat, drink, get her the fuck out"

"I will, don't worry. I don't want her here as much as you"

"Yeah, well, she is here, so just get it over with. Here, you can take these out yourself" he said, placing the drinks on a tray

"Ok" I picked up the tray and walked out to find Helen.

She was sat out in the sun, furiously texting away on her phone.

"Drinks" I said, as I walked out. She hurriedly put her phone away, like she was caught doing something bad. Weird.

I handed her the cappuccino.

"Thanks" She put the drink down.

"What did you want to eat?" I asked.

"Oh, erm just a ham sandwich or something"

"Ok, I'll go let him know" I walked off and gave Steve the order.

"I hope she chokes on it" was his response as I walked back out.

I sat back down, and took a sip of my latte. The silence was uncomfortable. I didn't know what to say, and part of me just didn't want to say anything to her. She broke the silence.

"Steve seems angry"

"Can you blame him?"

"Cheap shot" she said, her voice tinged with anger.
"Can you?" I persisted.
"No, I guess not" she conceded.
"Were you expecting open arms? Hugs, Kisses?"
"Don't be cruel, it doesn't suit you"
"No cruelty intended, just being realistic" I said.
"You always were very logical Jack" she said "Typical Engineer I suppose"
I didn't respond.
"He's very protective of you"
"He's a good friend, the only one I have left" I said.
"Another cheap shot"
"Another reality" I retorted. "Why are we here?"
Before she could respond, Steve walked out, placed the plates on the table, and walked off.
"It was a mistake coming here" she said softly "I'm sorry if it put you in an awkward position.
"He's a big lad, he'll get over it" I said.
"I wanted to talk about the kids"
And there it was. Boom. What the fuck was there to talk about?
I thought we were here because of the meeting this morning?
"I guess we are" she said "But I wanted to just chat about both kids in general"
Fuck sake you prick, keep it in your head.
"What about them?" I asked, defensively. Also worried.
"James hates me. He doesn't want to live with me does he?" she said.
"No"
She was expecting more, but she wasn't going to get it.
"Oh, ok" That threw her, she took a moment to compose herself.
I ate half of my sandwich, the silence was stupendous.
"He's angry because we moved away, I know. Not like I had much of a choice though right?" She looked at me, waiting for me to agree.

"Ok" I said, simply.

"Fuck sake Jack, you're not making this easy. You really have nothing more to say than Ok?" she hissed.

"No, not really. What the fuck are you expecting from me? Sympathy? *You* made this happen Helen. *You* did. Not me, *you*. Don't expect me to feel sorry for you because your relationship is going down the toilet? Again"

"What? How?" she started.

"Just a guess" I said.

"Schadenfreude, nice" she said.

"You think I take pleasure in it? The fact that my kids have to go through the upheaval of yet another separation?"

"You don't seem empathic about it"

"I couldn't give a rat's arse about what happens to you. The thing that makes me angry is the impact on the kids"

"You think I don't?"

"Do you?" I asked.

"What? Of course I do. But I'm entitled to a life Jack, I have a right to be happy"

"A right?"

"Yes. A right. Am I not allowed to be happy? You're all shacked up with little Miss Perfect, I'm entitled to do the same"

"Careful" I warned.

"Careful? What for?"

I took a breath. Stay calm. "I would still be married and we would still be a family if it weren't for you running of with gym boy. You have any idea what that did to the kids?"

She hung her head and remained silent.

"You have no right to comment on my personal life, or on my partner. We wouldn't be in this position if it weren't for you"

My heart was beating like a jack hammer, I could hear it in my voice. *Jack, we have a problem…*

"I'm trying my best. I'm trying to make a life for me and the…"

Her voice faded into silence, and the world with it. Darkness.

"Jack? Jack? Steve!" yelling, panic. I couldn't hear it of course, but that's what happened. Helen went into full panic mode, thinking I'd had a heart attack or something.
Steve came running out "What?"
"Jack" she yelled, lifting my head.
"For fuck sake, not again" Steve said, and pushed her aside.
He sat me up. "Jack, hey buddy, come on, wake up" The world slowly came back. Sound faded in, light filtered in through my eyes. "There you go. You ok brother?"
"Hmmm? Yeah, I'm ok" I said, still phasing back into reality.
"Jesus, what happened? You scared the shit out of me" Helen said, close to tears.
Steve snapped his head around to her "This is what you've done to him." There was venom in his voice, which was unlike him.
"What?" she said, confused "What happened?"
"You fucked up his mind is what happened" Steve said "Happy now?"
"Mate, its ok" I said.
"No, it's not ok. You have any idea what he's been through since you fucked off and left him? He's been through fucking hell is what. His mind is completely fucked up, he's a wreck. And it's all your fucking fault"
"Mate" I said. He turned towards me. "It's ok, I'm fine"
"But, she…"
"Mate, its fine, just leave it. Please?"
He thought for a second, then stood and left.
Helen was silent. Unsure what to do or say.
"Sorry about that" I said.
"What happened?"
"I fainted. It's been happening for a while"
"You're ill? Seen a doctor?"

"I have the occasional spells of low blood pressure, exasperated by mental health issues. Means I faint when I'm under pressure or in distress. I'm seeing a doctor and a counselor"
"Jesus. Can't they give you medication?"
"They will, and the counseling is helping"
"I had no idea" she muttered.
"Why would you? Like everything else, I'm dealing with it"
"You should have told me"
I looked confused. "Why? I told Chrissy, and we're dealing with it."
"Ok. How long has it been happening?"
"Have a guess" I said, and she hung her head.
"I'm sorry" she offered. I wasn't in the mood to go further into it.
"Ok. So, there's nothing I can do about James. He resents you for destroying his family, and doesn't like being away from his friends, it's a big part of his life. Elsie is hopefully dealt with now. Is there anything else you wanted to talk about?"
"No"
"Ok, well, in that case, I've got to get back to work." I got up, and left her.
I paid Steve on my way out; he apologised. I told him he had nothing to apologise for, and I would call him later.
I closed the door behind me, walked around the corner into the alleyway, and let it all out. I dropped to my knees. All the anxiety came rushing out. Tears came flooding, and I was shaking uncontrollably. I tried to steady my breathing, but to no avail; I need to let it run its course.
A few minutes later, I stood up, composed myself, and turned to walk back to the office. Helen was stood watching me from the top of the alley. She was crying. When our eyes met, she hurriedly turned and walked off. Fuck. I hadn't wanted her to see that. *She doesn't deserve to see you like that, vulnerable and broken*. No, she doesn't. *Bitch*.

I text Kyle to tell him I wouldn't be back in, then went home. I got in, found Chrissy sat on the sofa, lay my head in her lap, and fell asleep with her stroking my head. Safe.

When I woke up, I found Chrissy had been replaced by a cushion. I sat up, and looked at my watch; it was almost four o'clock. I could hear her upstairs on the phone to someone. I went to make a cup of tea. What a day. Terrible fucking day. I felt drained, embarrassed, ashamed, angry, confused. A proper melting pot of emotions. I put the kettle on, and got two mugs out. Whilst it was boiling, I did a bp test. Still low. I noted it on the chart, and brewed the tea.

Let's take a breather whilst the tea brews and analyse what just happened.
Wow. A right fuck up. I should never have agreed to the meeting. I wasn't ready for that kind of animosity. I hadn't felt that anxious or wound up in a long time. Can I blame Steve for his outburst? No. Of course not. Like me, he had a lot of pent up anger and frustration to vent. It needed to be said. You been in a similar situation ever? Fucking scary right? I hadn't intended to explode at Helen, hadn't even crossed my mind. She just pressed the right combination of buttons to set it off. I didn't want her to know any of the issues I was having. It was none of her business, and I still regret it all coming out like that. She had no right to know. I was angry with myself for a long time after that. Still am to be honest. I've had meetings with her since then, as parents, school stuff etc. I never know what to say. And like I said, I don't really want to say anything. I have nothing to say to her. Meeting her is always a nightmare; I'm anxious as fuck. I obviously come across as being rude or just ignorant, but I don't really care. I don't want to see her, let alone meet up with her. That's what texting is for. My safety blanket. How does she feel about it? Couldn't care less to be honest. You agree? Disagree?

Shrug. I don't know. It's just a weird situation every time. Parent evenings are terrible; she always tries to make conversation, but I'm just not interested. It's not great for the kids, but fortunately for me, they hang around me the whole evening, giving her minimal attention.

Anyways, erm, tea is ready. Ok. I poured tea, and took a mug and some biccies up to Chrissy. She blew me a kiss, and indicated she'd be about another twenty minutes.
I went back down, dunked some choc hob-knobs in my tea for comfort, and waited for her to finish. Half a packet later, she came down.
"Wow, looks like I showed up just in time" she said, nodding at the half eaten packet.
"I needed chocolate" I said.
"What a girly thing to say" she laughed, and sat down. "So, I assume it went badly?"
"I fainted in front of her"
"Jack!"
"Hey, I couldn't help it. She wound me up, and I let loose"
"You did?" she smiled.
"Yeah, properly. Her current relationship is breaking up, and I told her I was worried about the impact on the kids. She went on about having a right to be happy, I just got angry. I blamed her for all the issues with the kids, with me"
"Then what? What did she say??"
"Then I fainted"
"Fucking hell Jack"
"In a way, it was funny. She was terrified, thought I was having a heart attack. She called Steve out, who helped me up and sorted me out"
"I bet Steve was happy having her there"
"Yeah, like totally not. He gave me a barrage of abuse when I walked in"

"I bet" she laughed.

"And then he let loose on Helen"

"What? How? What did he say?"

"He blamed her for everything that was wrong with me, had a proper go at her"

"He's a good friend"

"Yeah, he is. I calmed him down, and he left us to it. I then had to explain exactly what was wrong with me"

"How'd she react?"

"I think she got the point"

"And then?"

"I left"

"That's it?"

"Erm, not exactly"

"What?"

"I crashed out in the alley, full breakdown"

She took my hand and kissed it "That would explain the falling asleep"

"She saw it"

"What?"

"Yeah, when I sorted myself out and stood up, she was stood at the top of the alley, watching"

"Fuck"

"Fuck indeed"

"Did she say anything?"

"No. She was crying. As soon as we made eye contact, she turned and left"

"Fuck Sake! That makes me angry. She has no right to see you that way"

"I know, sorry"

"Hey, not your fault, that's not what I'm saying"

"I know, I'm as angry about it as you are, trust me."

"She likes you, you know? She called you little Miss perfect"

"What?"

I laughed "it's a compliment, trust me"
"Couldn't care less"
"I know, but I just find it funny"
"Good for you" she said, and punched my shoulder. *Deserved that.* Yeah, I did.
"Yeah you did"
I rubbed my shoulder "We good?"
"Of course we are. I'm more concerned about how you are"
"I'm drained."
"I bet"
"Pint?"
"Thought you'd never ask" she smiled, and we went off to the bar for a beer.
We spent the rest of the evening in there. Not drinking heavily, we just had fun. I flashed up the bbq, and we had bratwursts. Bliss.

In bed, I once again went over the day's events. I was glad it turned out the way it did for a couple of reasons:

1. She deserved to hear the truth from me.
2. I guess I wanted her to know what was wrong with me so she could see what she had done.
3. She deserved to be chewed out by Steve, he'd earned the right.

I needed distraction tonight, so a trip to 221B Baker Street was required. I heard a lot of the story before the world faded away for the night.

Notes:

You may be thinking: *Wow, erm, sudden ending to the day there mate.*

I did. On purpose.

I try to keep each day to about 8-9 pages.

This one got to almost 12, so I pulled stumps on it. Also almost 5700 words. If they were all like that, the book would be around 100k words.

Why does that matter?

Economics. The longer the book, the higher the cost of printing.

The first book is 81 pages, 37k words, and is £4.99.

The second book is 104 pages, 54k words, and costs £5.57.

More pages, more cost, lower chance of sales.

The third is 122 pages, 60k words, so will be more expensive again. This one? Probably more again.

Just for clarity; I don't make more money off them if they cost more to buy.

Day 10, Tuesday, 19th of June.

D-day +1. I woke when the alarm went off. This was going to be a normal, boring, uneventful day.
I got up, changed into my running gear, and went out for a run. I needed to setup my mind for a decent day, I didn't want to be hung up on what happened yesterday. The run did exactly that. I felt refreshed, and ready for the day. Blowing out of my arse, but happy. I sat out on the doorstep with some water to cool off, then went for a shower.

Here's my mental requirements for today:
I wanted to run, have a bite to eat, go to work, lose myself in editing, go home, have dinner, then go to bed. Simple.
Let's do it.

Run – check.

After showering, I dressed, and went to have breakfast with Chrissy. She was bright and cheery as always, and had made me some toast and coffee. We chatted for a bit about random stuff like shopping, cleaning, garden, then I went off to work. We had been blessed with nice weather the last few weeks, today was no exception. The sun was shining, not a cloud to be seen. The village looked pretty in the sunlight; the thatched roofs, whitewash cottages, cobbled pavements. Lovely. I felt lucky to be here.

Breakfast – check.
Go to work – check.

Kyle was already hard at work when I got in.

The kid was a machine. *Probably further ahead than you are slacker*. Yeah ok, I get it. I was right; I had a lot of catching up to do after yesterday, so had a quick chat with Kyle, and got lost in work.

Get lost in work – check.

Wait. Standby on that one. My phone buzzed. I picked up; Helen.
I got up, and went outside.
"Jack, I need some help"
"What is it?"
"So, erm, like you said yesterday, my relationship is over"
"Ok"
"I ended it last night"
"Ok"
"I have until the end of the day to find somewhere to live"
"Ah"
"Can you take the kids for a few days whilst I sort myself out?"
"I'll take them forever"
"A few days would be fine thanks"
"Ok"
"If I get their stuff to mum and dad's, can you pick them up from there this evening?"
"Ok"
"Can you say anything other than ok?"
"Yes"
"Ugh, whatever. They'll be ready at seven"
She dialed off.
Happiness! I couldn't imagine myself happier at that moment. My kids were coming home for a while! I called Chrissy.
Engaged. I sent her a precis message and said I'd call later.
Good mood engaged, I went back inside, and back to work.
Kyle was so engrossed, he hadn't even noticed that I'd left.
"You been somewhere?" he said, confused.

"Just outside to take a call"
"Ah, sorry, I didn't even notice"
"We're very alike you and I" I laughed.
"Yeah, I guess so. You want some tea? I need a break"
"Tea would be nice"
I sat down and checked my work; almost done with this one. Then only 12 to go. Sigh.
"Here" Kyle said, putting a mug of tea on my desk.
I picked it up, and took a sip. "Ah, nice. Thank you"
"Everything ok?" he asked.
"Everything is ace" I said "How are things with you?"
"Well, ok I suppose." he was instantly lost; not a conversationalist.
"You found a house?"
"Oh, yeah, we've looked at quite a few online. We have a few viewings booked in for Thursday, so I'll be out a lot of the day I'm afraid. If that's ok of course?"
"No need to ask, you go"
"Ah, yes. Of course. I'll pop in early to finish off, then will be out the rest of the day"
"Better" I winked. "You done your work already?"
"Almost, might actually finish tomorrow so won't have to come in Thursday at all"
"Wow, wish I was that quick" I said "I'll be here till Friday afternoon probably"
"Oh, I could help…" I cut him off.
"No, absolutely not. I've been out a lot this week, I need to catch up."
"If you're sure?"
"Absolutely, I'll clear up my own mess"
"Fair enough"
He showed me some of the houses on the internet, some of which looked fantastic. Wow, things have changed.

Used to be that you started off with a small place and worked your way up. He was going big from the get-go. Good for him.
"Nice places mate, all in nice, quiet places"
"Just what we want" he said "Away from big city noise and pollution"
"Its nice being away from the noise" I admitted "I don't miss it at all"
"That's where I want to get to" he smiled.
We chatted a little longer, then went back to work. I set myself a target of getting out by five, which meant I had quite a bit of work to do. It was going to be hard, but doable. I got to it.
"I'm off Jack, see you tomorrow"
I heard the words, but my brain took a few moments to connect them to reality. I looked up. Kyle had shut down, packed up, and was heading out the door.
"Oh, erm, yeah, see you tomorrow matey" I said. He laughed, and left me to it.
Wow, what time is it? I checked the clock; 16.43. I looked back at the screen. Hmmm, about half an hour to go. I decided to buckle down and finish the video. It took 25 minutes. I saved it, and shutdown. The office was quiet. Not even the peaceful humming of the computers. Nothing.
I grabbed my stuff, locked up, and went home.
On the way, I had a thought; you didn't call Chrissy. Shit. Oh well, I'd have to deal with the fallout when I got home. The sun was still shining nicely, and it was going to be a pleasant evening. Bbq. Definitely. The kids would love it.

"Hey you" Chrissy said as I walked in "You were going to call?"
"Yeah, I forgot, sorry"
"What's up?"
"You're not going to believe this" I said.
"Try me"

"I had a call from Helen earlier, she's broken up with the current Mr. Wonderful"
"Already? They only moved in together a short while ago"
"Yeah, already. Anyway, she's been told to get out basically, so asked if I could have the kids. If *we* could have the kids."
"Oh, why didn't you tell me that earlier? I could have gotten the place ready, done some shopping"
Uh-oh, she sounds angry. Me thinks you fucked up.
"I'm sorry, I forgot"
"You forgot? You could have just text me"
"Sorry, I wanted to tell you over the phone"
"Ugh, ok, well, never mind. It doesn't really matter now."
I wasn't sure what to say, so I said nothing.
"Right, let's get to work. What time they coming?"
"I've got to pick them up from my ex-in-laws at seven"
"Seven? That's not long! Shit. Bit more notice next time Jack"
I felt like I'd apologised enough, so didn't do it again. "I'll sort the bathroom and toilet out if you sort their rooms" I said.
"Ok, go on then" she said. I did as commanded; got the cleaning stuff and went to work.
She huffed about, muttering under her breath. I felt bad. I hadn't meant to not tell her, but I didn't get it across very well. I was going to say something, but thought better of it and carried on with my cleaning instead.
At half past six, we were in the kitchen, checking the cupboards and fridge. "Ok, we need shopping. Do we have time tonight?" She asked
"Don't think so, but we have enough to last tonight and breakfast in the morning. I'll do shopping on the way back from dropping them to school.
"I'll go with" she said and sat down with a loud sigh.
"I am sorry, you know?" I offered.
"I know, and I am too. I overreacted. I just like the place being perfect when they're here, you know?"

"I know, I do too. I would have finished earlier, but I'm miles behind on my work as it is"
"Can Kyle not help out?"
"Seems unfair. He's almost finished his share as he wants to finish tomorrow. They have house viewings Thursday and Friday"
"Ah, ok. You going to be able to finish in time?"
"Yeah, should do. Need to get proper stuck in tomorrow and Thursday though"
She kissed me. "And here's me losing my rag over something so trivial"
"It's not trivial, and I'm the one who's sorry for not telling you sooner"
"Truce?" she asked.
"Truce"
We sealed the deal with a long, passionate kiss. *Yeah! Fuck yeah!* No, no, no.
"Whoa! No time" I said. In truth, it was getting a bit hot. *Why is that a problem you fucking melt??*
"What?" she said, still caught in the moment
I tapped my watch "Gotta go pick them up"
"Ah, shit yeah. Come on, let's go"

Tangent.

Not about the story, but about the writing real quick if I may? Yesterday was a lot of writing. I've gotten to 20.30 today in only 3.5 pages. Even then, I've stopped, gone back, and padded it out a few times already. I talked about writing too much, and there being too many pages. Conversely, I don't want the days to be too short either. Hence this tangent, to add more padding.

We went out, got in the car, and went to drive off.
"Wait a minute" I said, stopping the car.

"What is it?" Chrissy said.
"I'm driving"
"Oh shit, I hadn't even noticed" she laughed. We go out and swapped seats.
"Right, ready?" she asked.
"Yep, hit it."
She drove off in the direction of Ramsey, and was soon asking for directions. "I've not been here before, you'll need to direct me"
"Ok, left up here" We turned left into a small estate, its roads sparsely interspersed with sizeable properties. Helen's dad had done alright for himself. He was a barrister, and had worked on some high profile cases for UK Government. He was still a valued advisor, and I supposed still pulling in a six figure salary. Good for him.
"Just on the right up here, by the gates."
"Holy crap, what a house! They must be doing alright for themselves" she said in awe.
"Yeah, her dad is quite successful" I explained.
I pressed the bell on the gate post, and after a short delay, the gates slowly opened.
"Proper posh" she said, and drove up to the house. Sounds impressive, but I should offer some perspective: it was a nice six bedroom, detached house, like a lot of the other houses surrounding it. But, it wasn't like a mansion or grand country house. It was fairly modest. The gates were a necessary evil after they had been burgled when they had first moved in. It was thought to have been something to do with revenge for a case he'd worked on, but I don't think it was ever proven. He'd had the wall and gates put up immediately afterwards.
"I'll wait in the car" Chrissy said as we stopped outside.
"Ok, I won't be long" I jumped out, and walked up to the door, which opened as I approached. Her dad stuck out his hand "Nice to see you Jack" he smiled. I shook his hand "Hi Phil"

He bent down and waved to Chrissy "Hi Christelle". She smiled, and waved back "Hi Phil"
"The kids are ready, I think they're out in the garden, give me a minute, I'll go get them."
He turned to leave, then stopped and turned back to me. "Sorry Jack, I'm just assuming you wouldn't want to come in, forgive me"
"It's ok Phil, I'm happy to wait here" I smiled.
"Sorry anyway." he said, then went off to get the kids. No sign of her mother; suited me. I had nothing to say to her anyway.
Phil returned a couple of minutes later, laden with bags
"Gimme a hand would you Jack?" he said, handing bags over. We walked over to the car and put them all in the boot.
"Pfew, thanks Jack. They're just saying bye to grandma"
"No problem"
"Actually, I just wanted to say something if I may?" he said awkwardly.
"Sure"
I'm sorry how things have turned out, and make no apologies for Helen; she's a grown woman, responsible for her own mistakes in life. I 'm very happy to see you doing ok Jack, I mean that"
"Thank you Phil, that means a lot"
"You guys seem happy" he said nodding to Chrissy "That's good Jack, I hope it stays that way. You deserve happiness"
"Thanks" Weird, but heartfelt. You couldn't help but like Phil, he was such a genuinely nice guy. What he was doing married to her I didn't know. But hey, to each their own eh.
Not sure what else to say, I was silent. Thankfully saved by Elsie running out shouting "Daddy!"
She ran up and jumped into my arms "Whoa! Hey Ello" She clung on, as if for dear life.
"I missed you daddy"
"I missed you to sweet heart"

I put her down, and she ran off to see Chrissy. James followed a moment later. Bit more restrained, but his hug felt equally desperate. "Hey dad"

"Hey buddy" He was hugging tight, all his relief showing. He'd wanted this to happen.

"Hey guys, come on, say bye to grandad" I said, they did so, and I shook his hand before getting in the car. He leaned down through the window. "You be good for your dad and Christelle now you hear?"

"We will grandad" Elsie said from the back seat.

"Take care Jack, Christelle. Nice to see you both" And with that, he was gone. We drove down towards the gate, which opened automatically. I caught a glimpse of Phil still standing on the driveway as the gates closed behind us. He looked desperately sad.

"Bbq for dinner?" I said as we drove home.

"Yeah, nice" James said. Elsie agreed.

"Good. You guys can unpack whilst we get dinner ready. You have homework?"

"All done" James said.

"Genius"

"He seem alright to you?" Chrissy asked.

"Who? Phil?"

"Yeah, he was watching us go, still standing there as the gates shut"

"Yeah, I saw. Dunno, he looked sad. Maybe because of Helen and the loss of family cohesion?"

"Hmm, yeah, maybe." She shrugged it off and kept driving. In the back of my mind however, the gears were turning. And turning. Something was up, I saw it in his eyes. *Forget about it!* Yeah, you're right. I locked it away in a small, dark room in my mind.

You may at this point be thinking one or two things:

1. *Dinner after 1900??* Yes.
2. *WTF do you care what is going on with your ex-father in law?* He's a nice guy. What are you expecting? Should I automatically hate her entire family? We got on extremely well before the divorce, that doesn't just go away.

We got back to the house, and I went straight out to do the bbq. Nothing fancy, sausages and burgers. James joined me after he'd dumped his stuff. "Can I help?" he said.

"Here" I said, handing him the tongs "Look after this, I'll go get the rolls"

I handed over the manly responsibility to my son, and went into the kitchen. "How's it going?" Chrissy asked.

"Good, James is happy" I said, smiling "I just came in to get the rolls"

"Rolls? I've got some nice baps here instead if you're interested" she winked.

Fuck yeah! "No argument here, they do look nice" I said, admiring the bread rolls on the plate.

"Baps? As in…?" she wiggled her chest. *The fuck is wrong with you? Melt.*

"I know what you meant" I winked, picked up the plate, and went back outside.

A tomato whizzed past my ear, missing me by a fraction.

"Whoa!"

"Dick"

"Dodged a bullet there dad" James sniggered.

"Yeah, tell me about it" He didn't know the half of it. Frustration is real!!!

We had a quick dinner, and the kids were I bed by half eight. Bit of a late one for Elsie on a school night, but it was a special occasion after all. After we'd cleared up, I sat at the kitchen table, and pulled out the laptop to do some work.

"Wow, burning the midnight oil?" Chrissy commented
"Yeah, I'm so far behind because of all the time off this week. I need all the time I can get to catch up"
She walked over, kissed me on the head, and went off to bed
"I'll leave you to it. Don't stay up too late"
"I won't" Bold statement. There was every chance I'd still be here when the sun rose.
Not happening fucknut, I need sleep. Yeah, fair one. I yawned and got to work.
What seemed like 20 minutes later (in reality almost 3 hours), inner voice started shouting obscenities at me, so I saved and shutdown. *Fuck me, at last.* You win. Bed it is. It was just after one o'clock. *Fuck sake man, only 5 hours of potential sleep.* Sorry.

After brushing my teeth, I crept into bed. I thought I'd made it, but Chrissy immediately cuddled into me, which told me I hadn't quite.
No chance of headphones tonight. *Don't need them, I'm fucked.* Inner voice was right. I closed my eyes, enjoying the feeling of Chrissy laying against me. I kissed her head; her hair smells like a summer's day. Bliss.
And with that, I faded to black.
Jack out.

Note.

Bit shorter, gotta keep that word count down, or my proof reader will kill me!

Day 11, Wednesday, 20th of June.

Wake up
No
Wake the fuck up!
No!
Bladder; go!
Fuck sake! Ok! Jesus.
Reluctantly (very much so) I opened my eyes. Chrissy was still asleep. What time is it for fuck sake? Slowly, careful not to wake her up, I turned over and checked the clock. What the actual..!? It's only four o'clock. *Yeah, but your bladder is full, and you need to get to work early so you can finish Friday.*
Struggling to wake up, I got out of bed and stumbled unsteadily towards the toilet. Ok, you're right on both counts, still early though, wanker. *You'll thank me later.* Whatever.
My bladder was extremely grateful for the voiding, and the temptation to just crawl into bed afterwards was thwarted by inner voice. Don't even fucking think about it? Ugh.
Still not quite awake, I dressed in the darkness of the hallway so as not to wake up Chrissy. Do I have time to eat something? Nope, you can get something from the café later. Man. Ok. I wrote a quick note for Chrissy, then grabbed my bag and went to the office.

Hey uh, you taking the kids to school? No, they get the bus.

It was weird getting to the office before Kyle. I went inside, turned the lights on, and flashed up my pc. After I'd made a quick coffee, I went to work. So much to do! I'd have to have a chat with Kyle about taking on someone else. I had been thinking about it for a while now.

Might actually have to put it into action. In the meantime, I had to get on with it myself.

Kyle was not at all surprised to find me already hard at work when he walked in at 7. "Morning Jack, playing catch-up?"

"Morning. Yeah, gotta get this done by Friday. Let's go for a coffee at nine, I have something I wanted to discuss with you"

"Ooh, intrigue" he smiled "No problem"

"Nothing bad, don't worry"

"Ok. You want tea?" he said, walking over to the kettle.

"No thanks mate, I have coffee" I picked up my mug and took a mouthful of freezing coffee. I spat it back out immediately.

He laughed "You sure?"

"Nah, I'll do without thanks"

"No worries" He turned back to finish getting his mug ready. I once more faded out into my own little world.

It must have been close to nine when I felt a tap on my shoulder.

"Huh?" I turned to see what was happening

"Almost nine Jack, just saying"

"Wow, yeah, thanks mate. Gimme two secs" I turned back and saved my work.

"Right, ready" I got up, grabbed my phone, and we made our way over to the café.

I had a sudden uneasy feeling in my stomach. Fuck. Steve. Was he still angry? Surely not, I mean, he doesn't hold grudges right? Right? Ugh, I was dreading it.

"You ok there?" Kyle asked as we walked.

"Oh, yeah, just a thing going on with Steve and I"

"Really?"

"Well, maybe, maybe not. We're about to find out" I took a moment, then opened the door.

Tinkle.

"Fuck off"
I turned to Kyle "Definitely"
"Morning Mr Fletcher" Kyle said, hesitantly.
"Morning Kyle, I didn't mean you, I meant that one" Indicating me.
"Ah, well, coffee for one then please" he sniggered.
"If he wants a coffee, he can make it himself" Steve said to Kyle
"I *am* here you know" I said, not masking my frustration.
"Stephen, stop being so childish" Willow berated from the kitchen.
"I'm not being childish" he retorted.
"Stephen!" she warned.
"Ugh. Ok fuckwit, what do you want?"
"A kiss?"
"Fuck you" then "Come here"
I walked around the counter straight into a bear hug.
"You're a prick for setting me up, but still my brother"
"Love you too man" I said.
"And you fucking left me with her"
"What?"
He released me "Yeah, she stayed on for like half hour after you left, trying to chat to me"
"Oh shit, sorry mate"
"You're an absolute fucking dick."
"I know"
"Good. Now fuck off and sit, I'll sort you out"
I laughed, patted him on the shoulder, and went out to find Kyle in the garden.
They say you only find a friend like him once in a lifetime. I was lucky I found him, and that he was still in my life. *No comment.*
Yeah, not needed.
Contentment.

"You kissed and made up?" Kyle said as I walked up.
"Yeah, all good" I sighed, and sat.
"He's a good friend"
"The best"
"You're lucky. It's good to have someone like him in your life"
"Yeah, I tell myself that all the time"
"Ok" he took a breath "What did you want to talk about?"
"Ah yeah, sorry. Like I said, nothing bad, just wanted to float an idea"
"Ok"
"I'm sure you've noticed that I struggle to keep up my end of the work load. And, this week has been a bit of a wakeup call. I'm not as fast as you, and will never be able to keep up and share the load 50-50"
"You want me to take on more? No problem"
"No, no, I wouldn't do that. I was thinking we could maybe take on someone"
"Hire in a new person?" he asked.
"Yeah, I think the books support it, I've run some sums with Chrissy, and it wouldn't cost us much"
"This is exactly why I showed reluctance to be a partner; I know nothing about the business side of things"
"Well, I guess we do kind of balance out then" I winked "What you think?"
"You sure we can handle it?"
"Yeah, comfortably. I'm projecting our workload to increase by about 40% by the end of the year, so it makes sense."
"Ok, let's do it"
"Excellent" I shook his hand. "Now then, next question…"
"Yes?" he said, uneasily.
"You know anyone?"
His relief was obvious "Oh. Yeah, I think so. There's a girl that was in my class, she lives over in Chatteris. She's good"

"As good as you?"
"Better"
"Wow. That going to pose a problem in the long run?"
"How so?"
"Will she get bored and leave?"
"Different circumstances"
"Oh?"
"I don't want to go into it too far, but she has a child, and is not doing too well at the moment"
"How so?"
"She struggles job wise."
"If she's better than you, surely the world is her oyster?"
"She's different Jack. On the spectrum, very much so. She wears ear defenders"
"Ah, that a problem?"
"Not for me, but I wouldn't expect her to work in the office though, she's not good around people"
"She can work from the moon as far as I'm concerned, as long as she works"
"Oh, she'll work. Trust me. And she'll want the job. She does nights at the Tesco at the moment"
"Ok. So what I'm hearing is this; she probably won't do a face to face interview?"
"No"
"Definitely?"
"Yeah, she won't do it"
I thought for a second. It sounded like the solution to our problem. No face to face interview though. Why is that a problem? Yeah, you're right.
"Ok. You happy to speak to her and set up a trial period?"
"You sure? Without an interview?"

"Yeah. Tell her we're happy she can work from home. We'll provide a laptop, do a trial period, and if that works, we'll set her up with a home office. She has a home? I'm making a lot of assumptions"

"Yes, she has a home. I think that would work. Are you sure you're ok with this?"

"Are you? Do you have faith in her?"

"I do"

"Good. I trust your judgment. You happy to set it up?"

"Yes. She'll be over the moon."

"Good" I smiled.

"You know, you have a way of enriching people's lives Jack. You're a good man"

"Thanks?" Whoa! I was much too modest to take a compliment like that.

He laughed "Take the compliment, you make a difference. It's rare in people"

"Thank you"

Steve turned up with our coffees, placing them on the table with a huff.

"You gents ready to order food, or shall I just use my fucking crystal ball to figure it out?"

"Usual please" I said.

"Can I get a chicken salad sandwich please Mr Fletcher?"

"Yes you can Kyle. But please, for the love of Jesus fucking Christ, stop calling me Mr Fletcher. Makes me feel old. Steve will do"

"Ok, sorry Steve"

"Better!" he smiled, and disappeared off to the kitchen.

"He's funny"

"Yeah, that he is" I said, smiling.

Comfortably fortified, we returned to the office and went back to work.

I got lost in my own little world, whilst Kyle called his friend about the job. I'd like to say it all went well, but I had no idea; I was zoned out. Later, when I'd re-surfaced, Kyle gave me the full run down.
"Sounds positive" I said.
"Yeah, she seemed very happy. Took some doing to get her on the phone though"
"You did well"
"I need to send her a few samples, outline the requirements, and provide her with a laptop."
"Excellent, not a problem. We have some new laptops in the back, give her one of those"
"Ok, will do. I'll put some stuff together and go see her today if that's ok?"
"You all finished?"
"Yeah, I finished earlier."
"Wow, effort. The sooner we get her on board, the better."
"Understood. I'm on it"
He went out to get the laptop, and load it with the required software. We put together a package of samples, and a few un-edited vids for her to practice on. At lunchtime, he was ready, and set off for Chatteris.
"Good luck partner"
"Thanks partner" he smiled, and left.
Silence. Fuck. I got up and put the stereo on, just for background noise. I had 3 videos left to do, two big ones and one medium one. Ok. You got this, easy right? Yeah…
I was tired. It had been a tough week mentally, and I was struggling to focus. I decided to go for a quick run to sort myself out. Treadmill will do. I changed, and ran 3k. 3k was enough, my mind cleared, and I was ready to go again. I had a cold shower after, and got back to work.

A ringing sound. *Snap out of it!* Ringing? Phone!

I stopped working, and answered it.

"Hello?"

"Jack, just me. Thought I'd give you a quick rundown of how it went" Kyle.

"Ah, yeah, great. Shoot"

"It went super well. She's up for it. She did one of the vids whilst I was there. Fantastic work. I told her we'd do a 4 week trial to see how it goes"

"Sounds good so far"

"She agreed to the trial, but will keep working at Tesco until the end of the trial, just in case."

"Makes sense. One question?"

"Yes?"

"She has a name?"

"She does."

"Which is……"

"Oh, yeah, Irene"

"Irene..?"

He hesitated. "Holmes"

I almost swore "You gotta be kidding?"

"I know. But, yes, that's her name. Irene Holmes"

"Holy crap" I laughed "Sorry, not laughing at her, but you know what I mean right?"

"I get it. Irene Adler? Sherlock Homes? *The* woman?" he said

"She changed her name as soon as she hit 18, MASSIVE Sherlock fan"

"Wow. She's a keeper, just for the name!" I said.

"She also produces good work?"

"Yeah, sorry. What was her name before?"

"Melanie Dalton. I do have more news"

"Oh?"

"If the trial period goes well, she wants to meet you before signing anything"

"Wow. That must be a big deal for her"

"Yes, it is."
"Why?"
"Why what?"
"Why does she want to meet me?"
"I told her what you did for me, and that you're a Holmes fan. She wanted to meet you"
"Nice, I look forward to it"
"That's why she wanted to take the job"
"Because I'm a Holmes fan? Wow, cool"
"Yeah I guess. Hey, gotta go, see you Monday, have a great weekend Jack"
"You too partner"
I dialed off. Wow, Irene Holmes. Genius. I couldn't wait to meet this girl.
In a great mood, I got back to work, and managed to get both big videos finished by five.
With only a medium video left, I would easily finish tomorrow. Result.

"Get the fuck out"
"No, seriously, that's her name" I was telling Chrissy after I got home.
"Genius" she laughed.
"I know right" I said "She's extremely good apparently, according to Kyle"
"Well, I'm sure he would know"
"Yeah, I trust his judgment"
"Good"
"How was your day?" I said.
"Oh, you know, meeting after meeting. I have taken on a new case, lots to go over"
"Wow, sounds exciting"
"You taking the piss Beckett?"
"No, I'm being serious" I protested.

"Hmm, ok then."

"What's it about? Don't think I've ever asked about any of your work before"

"No, you haven't. Can't blame you mind. You really interested?"

"Yep, tell me about it"

"Ok. Can't tell anyone though"

"Look at where we live, who am I going to tell?"

"Good point. Ok, I'm investigating the Metropolitan Police"

"Wow, for what?"

"Financial stuff. They think some people are stealing money from budgets meant to support police work. I've been asked to look through the books and see if I can figure out how much, and who. If I can that is"

"Wow, that sounds proper exciting"

"Exciting is one word for it. It never gets exciting. Well, not your definition of exciting anyway"

"Sounds intriguing then"

"Better. Yeah it does right? Proper cloak and dagger"

"Far more interesting than what I'm doing, for sure. Although, I did a video on Jazzmasters the other day, which got me thinking I needed another guitar"

"Jazzmasters? As in musicians?"

"No" I laughed "It's a type of guitar, proper cool looking."

"Ah, I see. Why don't you get yourself one then?"

"I might well do that"

"You should treat yourself Jack, you work hard enough for it"

"Maybe"

"I'll be going down to London a few times for this case, you could come with sometime and check out the music stores"

"You know what? I like that idea"

"Me too, I hate travelling alone. Done that for far too many years"

I leant over and kissed her "Don't have to worry about that anymore"
"I know" she smiled "Speaking of which, are you ok with me disappearing into the city on Saturday?"
"Yeah, sure. Why wouldn't I be?"
"Well, the kids I suppose"
"Don't worry about that, I'll be at a footie tournament with them most of the day"
"Really? Shit. You want me to reschedule?"
"Nah, it's not nearly as exciting as it sounds, trust me."
"Sure?"
"Yeah, you go have fun with Willow, she probably needs it after dealing with Steve"
"Oh?"
I told her about Helen staying on after I'd left, and how pissed off he was when I went in for breakfast with Kyle earlier.
"Wow, proper grumpy pants"
"Yeah, we made up though"
"Good, seems weird, you guys not talking. Can't imagine it"
"Me neither. Hey were you ok with the kids this morning? Sorry, I just had to get into work early to stand a chance of finishing all my work this week"
She waved her hand in a dismissive gesture "Yeah, it was cool, I enjoyed it" she smiled.
"Good. Hopefully won't happen again with our new starter"
"Can't get over that name, genius" she giggled
"Yeah, just be careful not to laugh in front of her eh"
"I won't silly"
"Hmm. How are the terrible twosome? They're upstairs I assume?"
"Yeah, they're fine, both came home extremely happy and disappeared off upstairs"

"Good" It made me happy to know the kids loved being here. If only I could have them all the time. Sigh. Never going to happen. Oh well. I went up so find my treasures and to find out how their days had been.
"I'll do dinner. Salmon pasta ok?" Chrissy yelled after me
"Wow, yeah, perfect" I said, giving her a double thumbs up.

I found Elsie busy texting her friends, listening to music.
"Hey you, how was your day?"
"Daddy!" she ran over and gave me a massive hug. "I've had a great day thanks"
"You have?" I was worried about this one, and hadn't heard back from the headmaster yet.
"Yep, it was good"
"No more trouble?" I asked carefully.
"No, they weren't in today"
I kissed her head "Good"
She gave me another hug "Thank you daddy"
"Anything for you my angel. What you listening to?"
Not gonna lie; I hadn't heard of whoever it was she was listening to. I must be getting old…

After spending a few more minutes chatting to Ello, I went off to find my boy. I knocked on his door, and waited for him to open. Yeah, it's a thing once your kids get a bit older; privacy. You appreciated it when you were a teenager right? Respect their needs.
"Hey dad" he said, hugging me. Yeah, if you hadn't noticed already in the previous 3 books, we're big on hugging. I was extremely keen to ensure my kids weren't afraid to show affection.
"Hey buddy, how's things?"
"All good" he smiled "I'm glad we're here"
"Yeah, me too man. Me too"

At least I knew the music he was listening to, a little of his old man had rubbed off on him; Hendrix. I was proud. If only I could get him to pick up a guitar…
We chatted for a while about school, but mostly about football. He was really looking forward to the tournament at the weekend, and was happy he was here as he would at least be able to get to it. Although, I'm sure his mother would have taken him. She didn't really enjoy sports though, so didn't have the ability to bond with him over it. Bonus points for me I guess.
We made it about halfway through Bold as Love, when Chrissy shouted up that dinner was ready.
"I'll go set the table" James said, jumping up. Wow, keen…
Dinner was marvelous, delicious, awesome, and many more words that mean goodness. She was a hell of a cook. What a woman! Yeah, had to fit that in somewhere right?

After we'd cleared away and done the dishes, we settled down in the living room and watched a movie. James had the choice tonight, and we ended up watching Dead Poets Society.
Bit highbrow for Elsie I thought, but, bless her, she sat through it. She even joined in with the barbaric yalping!
My boy takes after me so much. DPS was one of my favourite movies; I'd watched it countless times as a teenager. That, and Spaceballs of course…
They went to bed happy. I can't put into words how extremely happy I was. I know we're over-using the word "happy" a bit here, but I just was. Extremely happy. To the point of tears. My kids were home. If only for a week. I didn't care. They were here and I was absolutely fucking loving it.
It must have been obvious, because: "Hey, you crying there Beckett?"
I wiped my eyes "Yeah, sorry"
"You ok"
"I'm just so happy" (there it is again!)

"Bless you, come here" she held her arms out, and I fell into them. It was like falling into a field full of lavender. The smell of her perfume was both intoxicating and soothing. I was in danger of falling asleep here! *Hey, I can think of worse places!* Perv.
"Tell inner voice to do one, we're enjoying the moment" Chrissy said. *Ok, point taken lady…*
It was pure bliss. I lay there for as long as I could before I started nodding off. She patted me on the shoulder "Come on you, let's have an early one. You could do with it"
"Yeah, I could"
And so, we went off to bed for an early night. Not THAT kind of early night. There was sleeping.

As always, I went through the day's events in my head before putting my headphones in. It had been a hell of a day right? Ello had survived school, and actually had a great day.
Result. James was happy, and I got to take him to footie at the weekend. Result. I'd spoken to Kyle about taking on an assistant, and he had sorted it within hours. Result. I had made up with Steve. Result. I was in bed with the most beautiful woman in the world. Result. Wow, a day of results. Result. *Over using the word "result" now too dickhead!*
Fuck you man. I've got to go see Holmes and tell him all about Irene Holmes! Yeah! Boosh.

Day 12, Thursday, 21st of June.

"Jack!"
Shaking. Wtf?
"Jack, wake up"
I opened my eyes, Chrissy was shaking me, whispering into my ear with a degree of desperation.
"What?"
"Noises downstairs, listen…."
She was right, there were sounds downstairs. Cat? Nah, not likely. Kids? Unknown. What the fuck was it? There was a sudden loud crash accompanied by some very colourful whispering.
"What the fuck? That wasn't downstairs, that was outside" I whispered to Chrissy
"Outside? Go check"
More swearing from outside. "Fuck, shit, balls! Ouch!"
I looked at Chrissy "That's American"
I got out of bed, and went over to the window. I carefully opened it, being as quiet as possible. Peered over the edge, and saw someone hobbling around on the drive, still swearing like a trooper. Definitely a yank, and female.
"Oi!" I shouted down "What's going on?"
"Oh shit, fuck" more stumbling, a fall, a scream. "Aargh! Motherfucker!" What the fuck is going on?
"Oh no" Chrissy said over my shoulder.
"What?"
"Shit, I know her"
"What?? Who the fuck is it? Its three o'clock in the fucking morning"
"Its my sister"
"Your sister? She's in America though isn't she?"

"Yes, supposed to be, but that's definitely her"

I moved out of the way to let her lean out the window "Fleur?"

"Hey sis" came the response from the bush she'd fallen into.

"What the fuck?" I mumbled.

She ran downstairs, and opened the door. I ran down after her, this was going to be good.

"Be careful, I think I broke something, its in my fucking foot and hurts like buggery"

"What?" Chrissy said.

"Oh, look out, she's knocked over the milk bottles, there's broken glass everywhere"

"Jesus Fleur" Chrissy yelled.

"Wait there, I'll get the brush" I went out to the back garden and retrieved the brush. I pushed past Chrissy and went out, brushing as I went. "Pop the light on" I said to Chrissy. She obliged.

"Holy shit" came the cry from the bush "That's bright as fuck"

I finished brushing all the glass out of the way, and let Chrissy know "Ok, all clear"

Se darted out to help her sister out of the bushes.

"One, two, three!" with a big pull, she managed to extricate her sister from her predicament.

"Hey sis" Fleur said, falling into her arms.

"Hey you" they hugged for a bit, then separated, with a "What the fuck are you doing here at three in the morning?"

"I'm so sorry, I totally fucked up massively"

"What are you doing here? Where's Jeff?"

"Ugh, don't get me started. Jeff is fuck knows where"

"Come on, let's get you in, careful now"

I helped her get her sister into the kitchen, and got the first aid kit out.

"Hi" she said, holding out her hand "You must be Jack"

"Hope so. You must be Fleur" I said, shaking her hand "Hell of an entrance"

"I'm so embarrassed. I was going to leave a note and get a hotel somewhere, then I tripped over those bottles and fucked everything up"

"It's cool" I said.

"You scared the shit out of us" Chrissy added "Let me look at that foot. Oh Jesus Fleur look at it"

"I'd rather not, can you bandage it up?" she winced.

"Yeah, I can. Sit still"

"I'm so sorry" she said, bursting into tears.

"Hey, its ok, no harm done" I said, trying to reassure her. I had the wrong end of the stick though. *Yeah, you do.* She's not upset about this situation. *Nope.* Husband? *Yep.*

"What's he done now?" Chrissy asked angrily. Obviously history there…

"He's fucking his fucking yoga teacher" she blurted out. She's got a hell of a mouth on her eh.

Chrissy continued to dress her foot and comfort her at the same time. I took a moment to get a good look at Fleur. While they looked a lot alike, Chrissy was deffo ahead in the looks. *Close though, she's fit aint she?* Wow. *You said they look alike.* They do. *By definition she's fit then right?* Ugh, whatever.

Things were calming down a bit between the sisters, which was good. "Tea anyone?"

"Would you mind?" Chrissy asked.

"No, of course not. Fleur?"

"Yes please" she said. She was desperately trying to compose herself. "Oh gosh, I must look a mess"

"I've seen worse" I said. No wait that wasn't me. You absolute fucking penis. *Hehehehehe…*

"What?" both sisters turned to me.

"Eh? What?" I said, innocently.

"Inner voice is a dick" Chrissy said, shaking her head in disgust.

"What?" her sister said, confused.

"Never mind, I'll tell you about it tomorrow."

Off the hook! You are still a complete fucking arsewipe.
I skulked off to make a pot of tea. Still chastising inner fucking voice in my head.
We sat for a while, with a cup of tea, before I left the sisters to it and went to bed. My input here was minimal, so I made my excuses.
"Hey Jack" Fleur said "I'm really sorry, this didn't go how I wanted it to. You must think I'm a mess"
"Don't worry about it. I'll get you some blankets and a pillow and pull the sofa bed out in the living room for the time being"
"Thank you"
"Like I said, not a problem, good night"
"Good night"
I went upstairs, got the blankets and pillows from the airing cupboard, and made up the sofa bed in the living room. Wait, where's her suitcase? I went outside, and found it on the drive. I sighed, and put it in the living room. It weighed a fucking tonne. Exhausted, I went to bed at 03.55.
What a fucking night.
Didn't take long to fall asleep, didn't notice Chrissy get back into bed. I was out.

Until my fucking alarm sounded that is.
"Fucknation" I reached out and silenced it. Fuck. Time to get up already.
I turned over. Oh. She's up already. Of course she is. Fuck sake, I'm tired. Very reluctantly, I got out of bed and staggered straight into the bathroom and showered. Inner voice was being a knob.
Should be an interesting morning.
Yeah, should be.
Her sister is hot.
Jesus man, give it a rest.
Like you hadn't noticed…

Sigh.

Shower was working, but I could feel it was going to be a long day. Hopefully I could fit in a nap sometime.

At work

What?

Just you at work, know what I mean?

Hmmm, yeah. Ok.

Good lad.

For once, inner voice made a good point; I could sleep in work. I had one vid left, which would probably take me till lunch, then I could catch a few hours of Z time. Instantly cheered up, I dried and dressed. *For once? I've bailed you out plenty of times!*

Meanwhile, in the kitchen, the kids were already up, and were sat chatting excitedly to their new family member.

"Morning" I said, walking in.

"Morning daddy" Ello said, and gave me a hug.

"Morning Jack" Fleur said. "Hope you don't mind, I got up early and made breakfast"

I looked at the table; stacks of pancakes, fresh fruit, juice, coffee.

She can fucking stay.

"Wow, no, not at all" I smiled.

"Good, sit, I'll pour coffee" I did as commanded, and took a cautious sip of coffee.

"Don't worry, I learned how to make coffee here, not in the US" Fleur winked.

"I erm…" I said. Busted. Whilst known for being big coffee drinkers, I've always found American coffee to be extremely weakly brewed. Not in this case though. Good.

"I know the coffee can suck in the US" she said "But I hope mine is ok"

"Perfect" I said. "Where's Chrissy?"

"Oh, she's upstairs working, she had breakfast already"

"Ah, early start eh. Well, this all looks fantastic" I said, tucking in.
"Good" she smiled "My way of apologising. Sorry about last night, not my proudest moment"
"Don't worry about it. How's your foot?"
"Well, I can walk on it, so I don't think it's as bad as it looked"
"Great" I smiled.
The rest of breakfast was taken up by the kids asking 101 questions about Fleur, and living in America. I took a back seat, and enjoyed the moment. The kids were loving having this exotic, mysterious woman in the house. *So am I.* Shush.

After the kids had disappeared upstairs, I was left with Fleur. On my own. *Fuck yeah!* Shut up.
"So, Jack, I've heard so much about you, I feel like I've known you all my life"
"Ok..." I said
"You make her happy" she smiled.
"I hope so, she makes me happy for sure"
"You seem like a good guy"
Ah, I see what's going on here; older sister looking after her younger sibling...
"I like to think so"
"I get good vibes from you" she smiled "And, you're kids are fucking adorable"
Her accent was weird, sort of half English, half American. *It's hot.* Jesus, will you fuck off.
"Thank you"
"So, Chrissy tells me you haven't done it yet"
I almost spat out my coffee. "She did?" What the fuck?
"Yeah. You're a really understanding guy Jack, well done. She had a bad time of it"
"We both have our reasons" I said.

"Ah, yeah, the divorce. Sorry. Though I may be asking for advice soon" she winked.
"It's not a pleasant thing to go through"
"I know, sorry, I didn't mean to make a joke out of it"
"It's cool."
"Hey, you mind if I use the shower? I feel like shit, and a shower would help"
"Of course, help yourself"
"Thank you Jack, I really appreciate your being so good about all of this"
"Trust me, the breakfast made up for it" I smiled.
She disappeared off upstairs, and I finished eating in silence.
She's a cracker. She's certainly something.
The kids helped me clear up before they both disappeared off to school. I should get to work. I went up and carefully went into the office; Chrissy was on a call, so I just kissed her head and went off to work.

Ah, fresh air. It was lovely out, though they said it may rain later on. Didn't look like it at the moment. It was unusual for me to be in the office alone, and I didn't really like it. I liked Kyle's company, we were very alike. It made me smile. But, it gives me the opportunity to have a nap later on. That also made me smile. I booted up, and went to work.
One medium sized video to do. It was an instructional vid, about musical theory I knew nothing about. I still knew nothing about it by the time I finished it. But, it was done. I clicked Send, and shut down. Time check; 11.23. I may have an early lunch, THEN have a nap. *Good thinking Jacko.*

Tinkle

"Oh for fuck sake. I was just telling the girls I was having a good day. Then you walk in."

The girls in question, in their 70's, both giggled and walked off to their table.
"Hey man" I said "Thanks for the warm welcome"
"Anytime dick face. What can I get you?"
"Decaf latte please, and something to eat"
"What the actual fuck? Decaf?" he leaned across the counter, and felt my forehead "You feeling ok?"
"Funny. I'm tired as fuck. I just want a hot drink, then I'm going back to the office for a nap, so caffeine is the last thing I want"
"Oh, knackered eh? Something to share with the group?"
"No, not like that." I told him all about the night's events as he very theatrically pretended to blow the dust off a bag of decaf beans.
"Fucking hell lad, I didn't even know she had a sister. No wonder you're fucking knackered"
"Yeah, tell me about it."
"Have a seat, I'll sort you out"
I plonked myself down in a window seat. Man, I was tired. Though I hadn't really been up that long last night, I was completely fucked. My bp was not where it should be, but it was rising. Having the kids around was doing me the world of good. Both mentally, and physically. I knew the dream would still be over, but chose not to think about that for the time being. I had an appointment booked with Pam next Friday, and I hoped to be fully refreshed and recharged after our trip to Italy. The trip. Wow, the trip. I was looking forward to it, it would be good to get away from all this, and just relax somewhere in the sun with good food and wine. Bliss.
"Bliss?"
"What?"
"You said bliss"
"I did?"
"Yeah, you did" Steve said, placing a tray in front of me.
"Oh, I was just thinking about the holiday" I explained.

"Ah, I see. Not talking to yourself then?"
"Hmmm. Maybe"
He ruffled my hair "Nutjob"
"Certified"
"You got that ring yet?"
"No, not yet" Shit. The ring.

Tangent.

Not about the ring. Something was brought to my attention the other day; I made a statement in book 2 as follows:
"The difference is that she changed *You*. The very fundamentals that make you who you are. Your personality. Everything that makes you Jack Beckett has been changed. Forever. Regardless of how much therapy you get, or how much time passes, you can never get past the fact that your personality has changed. It stays forever. You can never be who you were before. You said it yourself in our first chat; you're superficially ok, but fundamentally sad."

Remember that? When Jack went to see Pam?
Got me thinking. Whilst true, I didn't want to intimate that you could never be happy with someone else. Does that make sense? You may have changes on the inside, but you're still capable of being happy in a relationship. Didn't want you to think you couldn't be. I am.
Ok, back to the ring...

Damnation and hellfire. I'd forgotten about the ring. I needed to get into the city. But when? Chrissy was going on Saturday, we're flying out Tuesday. Fuck.
"Earth to Jack?"
"Sorry, was just thinking about the ring. I haven't got it yet"
"Fuck me lad, you don't half zone out, you know that?"

"Yeah, I know"
"What the fuck you going to do? You even know what size ring to get?"
"THAT I do know. She wears her mum's engagement ring, so I measured it with a set of calipers"
"Of course you did…"
"Of course I did. Anyway, I need to get to the city. But Chrissy and Willow are in Saturday."
"Right?"
"When will I get the chance?"
"What you doing today?"
"Nothing"
"Exactly…"
"Genius."
"Obviously. Now eat up and get the fuck out."
"Yes Sir"
I ate my Danish and left.

Why hadn't I thought of that?
Yeah, dick head, why hadn't you?
Erm, why the fuck didn't you?
Good point.
Next problem…
What?
How you getting to PB?
Ah. Fuck. Bus?
Lol! Bus wanker!
Jesus… Fuck sake; I'd have to get a bus to Huntingdon, then a train into PB. I checked the timetable at the bus stop; 23 minutes. That gave me enough time to go back to the office to get my wallet. Cool.

Just over 2 hours later, I was stepping off the train onto Platform 1 in Peterborough station.

I had a plan; 3 jewelers, route mapped out. Should take a couple of hours. Let's go.
It wasn't busy, which suited me. I found what I was looking for in the second jewelers; a beautifully simple platinum ring set with a single diamond. It was perfect. Relief. Let's not talk about how much it cost…
I got a sandwich from Tesco for the journey home, but on impulse, decided to get a taxi back. Cost be damned, I just wanted to get home.
And so it was, that within 4 hours, I was sat in a taxi, chomping an egg & cress sarnie, with a ring in my pocket. Good work.
The cab dropped me to the office at just after half three. I was fucked. I went inside, set an alarm for five o'clock, and fell asleep on the sofa.

Ugh.
The alarm buzzed loudly.
Fuck sake. I silenced it. I was in a cracking dream about…
About… Fuck. Why is it you can never remember your dreams?
I stretched out, yawned loudly, and went to the toilet to splash some water on my face.
Better. I focused on the face staring back at me from the mirror. I looked like myself, just not as full of life as I used to be. There was an emptiness in my eyes. Did other people see that? I hoped not.
Wow. I sighed, and went home.

The house was bouncing when I got home; Chrissy and Elsie were in the kitchen, baking cupcakes, both singing along to some music or other. James was out with his girlfriend, and Fleur? No sign.
"Ladies" I said, loudly, to be heard over the music.
Chrissy jumped "Jesus! You scared the crap out of me"
"Daddy! We're making cakes"

"Ooh, nice, some for me I hope?"
"There will be plenty" Chrissy winked.
"Good" I said, rubbing my tummy "Where's Fleur?"
"She's gone off to PB to put flowers on mum and dads graves"
"Ah, ok" I said, no need to go further. *Why doesn't she ever go?* Shush.
"How was your day?"
"It was good thanks, did the last video, went to see Steve, and then had a nap"
"Nap??" she asked shocked.
"I'm knackered, I needed to sleep" I protested.
She laughed "Lightweight"
"Whatever, I just needed to sleep"
"Poor baby" she said, and went to kiss me. I pulled my head away.
"Ooh! Feisty" she laughed.
"I have feelings you know" I feigned "Somewhere"
They both laughed at this "Silly daddy"
I rolled my eyes and walked out. I was still feeling tired. *Run?* What? *Run? Might make you feel better?* Ok, why not. I got changed, let the ladies know, and headed out.

The weather was still holding, despite the warnings to the contrary from the Met Office. It was pretty quiet, but then I suppose it was dinner time. A few fishermen were sat on the bank of the canal, nodding off. I envied them. But, my body was too focused on running to feel tired. Other than the tiredness from the run itself. I got to the halfway point, and decided to push a little further.
Rebel! Don't get excited, I only want to add another kilometer. When I stopped my watch at the bridge, I had clocked 6.03k. Nice. Didn't actually feel much more tired than after a 5k. Result.

I walked back home, grabbed some water, and went out in the garden to cool off.

Chrissy and Fleur were there, beers in hand.

"Hello Mr Fitness" Fleur said, then to Chrissy "He really is a keeper"

"I know" Chrissy smiled "He's even got me running"

"What? Get outta here!"

"Yep, loving it" she smiled proudly.

"You? Exercising? Miracles will never cease!"

"Hey, don't make me out to be some kind of slob!"

"Me? Never!"

Sisters. Funny. "She's been doing really good" I added in her defence.

"See?"

"Good for you" she said, and they clinked their glasses together in salute. "What happened to the Cello?"

"Ach, I sold it, I was rubbish at it" Chrissy said, dismissively.

Good fucking point. I hadn't thought of that at all. What happened there? I decided I'd ask her later, when we were alone.

"Oh, ok" Fleur said, picking up on the icy tone.

"So, Fleur" I said, rapidly steering us in a different direction "How's the foot?"

"Oh, fine, just fine. Wasn't as bad as I thought. We changed the bandage earlier, and it looks ok"

"Good to hear"

"You'll be glad to hear I found a place to stay in Ramsey, I'll be moving there tomorrow, so just one more night with me I'm afraid"

I laughed "You can stay here as long as you need to, the kids will be going home…" I stopped. Fuck. Going home. Going home. *Jack!*

"Going home?" Fleur said.

"Oh shit" I heard Chrissy say dimly.

I tried to look at her, but her face faded into blackness.
A moment later, light started filtering back in, and sound faded back up.
"What the fuck just happened?" Fleur said, voice full of concern.
"Jack?" Chrissy said "Oh, you're back" Relief.
"What?" I offered meekly.
"You ok my darling?" Chrissy's hand on my face, comforting.
"Yes, I'm fine" I said, sitting up.
"Did you just pass out?" Fleur asked.
"Yes, apologies" I offered.
"Don't apologise, what happened?" Fleur responded.
Chrissy explained what had happened, and what was wrong with me.
"Oh wow, you poor thing"
"I'll be fine" I smiled "Honestly, it was only for a second or so"
Erm…
"A second? You were out for a good minute or so" Fleur said.
"What?" I looked at Chrissy, who nodded. "Wow"
"Maybe you should go for a lay down" Fleur suggested.
"I think she's right" Chrissy added.
I wasn't going to argue. "Ok, Good idea" I stood, slowly.
"I'll come with you and check your blood pressure" Chrissy said, taking my arm.

A few minutes later, we were sat on the bed, nurse Lenoir taking my bp.
"Ach Jack, it's still low. Not as low as it was, but still low." She unstrapped the monitor, filled out the sheet and told me to have a sleep. I was still in my running kit, but was in no state to argue. I lay down, and slept like a baby.

I woke with a start. Shit. How long had I been out for? I focussed in on my watch; it was 21.44.

Holy shit. I jumped up and went out to o a quick check on the kids; both safely in bed. Relief. Next, I had a shower as I smelled. When I'd dried off and dressed, I found Chrissy and Fleur giggling in the bar, singing along to the Spice Girls.
"Ladies" I said, walking in.
"Jack!" Chrissy giggled "Didn't expect to see you till the morning"
"So I see" There was a small collection of empty beer bottles, and coke cans, as they'd now moved on to Morgan Spiced…
"How are you feeling?" Fleur asked "Gave me a hell of a fucking shock"
"I'm good thanks. Mind if I join?"
"Of course not" Fleur said, and beckoned me in. "Have a beer"
The Spice Girls were just starting another song, this could be an interesting night…

We had a great time, laughter, singing. Just fantastic. Fleur was full of stories, but was very careful not to mention her husband. I'm sure the girls had talked about that already. I wasn't going to mention it. There were a couple of things I needed/wanted to talk about though:

1. The Cello.
Seems innocuous, but I was intrigued. It's such a beautiful sounding instrument. We'll find out.

2. Visiting Graves.
I'd not known her to visit her parents graves since she'd moved in. Unless she did it without telling me. Why would she not? Weird.
But, those could wait. I said goodnight, and left the singing sisters to it.
I had an appointment with Mr. Holmes; Lestrade had a new case we needed to check out.

Day 13, Friday, 22nd of June.

I had set my alarm a bit earlier than usual, as I wanted to get up and make breakfast for the kids. I felt bad for not having spent time with them yesterday. But I had achieved my main objective yesterday; I had the ring. Now I just had to do the hard part, and figure out when exactly I wanted to do it.
Concentrate. Kids. Ok. I got up, showered, dressed, and went down to get breakfast ready. They'd had pancakes yesterday, so I decided for simplicity; scrambled eggs on toast.
I made myself a coffee, and got to work. I was just buttering the toast when James appeared.
"Morning dad, smells good" he said, and poured himself some oj.
"Morning mate, you sleep ok?"
"Yeah, like a log" He seemed happy. *Of course he does, he's not at hers*. I know, but soon he would be. *Soon, but not just yet.*
"That's good" I smiled "Hope you're hungry"
"Starving" he replied, putting his glass down. "You still ok to take me to the footie tomorrow?"
"Of course, wouldn't miss it for the world"
"Sweet"
I plated him up a big portion and put it in front of him "Feast"
"Oh wow, nice one dad" he said, and tucked in.
The smell of food had also roused my youngest from her lair, and she appeared in the kitchen, rubbing her eyes.
"Morning Ello" I said, lifting her up and giving her a big squeeze.
"Morning daddy" Not quite as full of enthusiasm as James, she sounded tired. She probably still had disturbing dreams about the bullying. I hadn't heard back from the school, but I'll give it till lunch before I called them.

"Have a seat angel" I said, kissing her head.
James rubbed her back as she walked past. "Morning tiny"
She sat next to him and rested her head on his shoulders. It was a sweet moment. There weren't many of those anymore now James had gotten older. But, it was obvious he was protective of his sister. He'd demonstrated that Monday when he'd asked me to sort it before he got into trouble.
It was frustrating that I hadn't heard from the school yet. But I kept telling myself to give them till lunch. *Patience Jack.*
I plated up her breakfast and gave it to her. Smile said it all. Slowly but surely, my little girl came to life, and was soon back to her old self chatting about this and that. It was heart-warming.
Fleur joined us a few minutes later, likely woken by Elsie's chattering.
"Morning" big yawn. "Ugh, my head. You have any aspirin?"
"Ibuprofen" I said, heading to the cupboard to get some. I took out the pack, and gave it to her. She poured a glass of juice and popped two tabs. "Wow, I need food"
I laughed "Sit, I'll sort you out. You ok with scrambled eggs?"
"Honey, right now, I'm ok with anything, as long as its edible"
Giggles from Elsie, and a reserved laugh from James.
He fancies her.
What?
He fancies Chrissy, logic suggests he fancies her lookalike sister.
Fuck sake.
Yeah, you know it.
Was that another thing I needed to worry about? Hopefully not. He was still happy with his girlfriend, so even if he did like Fleur, it would probably stay as a secret little crush.
"Hey Ello, any of those cakes left from yesterday?" I asked, changing the subject in my mind…
"Yes, there are some in that container" She pointed to a Tupperware on top of the fridge.

"Nice, I'll have some with a cup of tea later" I winked.
"They're very nice" James added.
"I look forward to it then. Fleur, 2 rounds of toast?"
"Three please if that's ok?"
"Three it is" I smiled.
"Morning everyone" Chrissy said, walking in, she kissed the kids heads, then me, then sat next to Elsie. "Any of that breakfast heading my way?" she asked, winking at Elsie, who giggled.
"Yes dear, on its way" I said, playing along.
"You want coffee?" Fleur asked, pouring her own.
"Yes please"
She dutifully filled a mug for her little sister "Here you go, you want some of these?" she held up the ibuprofen.
"Nah, I'm good thanks"
"Ugh, you never did get a hangover, I'm so jealous" Fleur said, delicately.
"Lucky me" Chrissy smiled smugly.
"You guys want a ride to school?"
"I'm getting the bus with Tamsin" James said.
"Ooooh Tamsin!" Elsie teased.
"Ello" I said shaking my head "Leave him alone. Ok mate, no problem. Just you and me then young lady"
"Can I come? It's been a long time since I saw a school here" Fleur said.
I looked at Elsie, who said "Of course you can"
"Great. Go brush teeth and get ready then Ello"
She ran off, excited by the prospect of this strange lady coming with us.
I cleared up, and Fleur went off to have a quick shower as soon as Elsie emerged from the bathroom. I told her we'd be leaving in 15 minutes.
"Not a problem, I'll be ready in ten" she said, disappearing into the living room.

I cleared up, and sat waiting with a glass of oj, chatting to Chrissy.
"Can I ask a question?" I said.
"Uh-oh, ok…"
"The Cello, why?"
She looked at the floor for a moment, then looked at me
"Remember that prick I told you about?"
"Yes, the one we saw at Waitrose"
"Yeah. It was his. He lent it to me to try. You know, before I bought my own"
"Ah, ok"
"I know I shouldn't have, but I smashed it up with a hammer and chucked it on his driveway"
I burst out laughing.
"What's funny?" she asked.
"That's WAY better than selling it"
"A waste of an innocent instrument"
"Well, yeah, but cool though" I kissed her "I would have done the same"
"You would?"
"Oh fuck yeah. Sadly, Helen didn't play an instrument"
"Hmmm, well, don't mention it to Fleur, she doesn't know"
"My lips are sealed" I said. I would have thought she would have confided in her sister at least. Bit weird. Oh well.
Fleur insisted on driving, so we went off to the school in her hire car. Not that anyone minded; it was a very nice Mercedes. We walked around to the entrance used by Elsie's year, and saw her off. As we turned to walk away, I heard my name.
"Jack!"
I turned to see who it was, and saw Mr Jackson waving at me from the other side of the playground. I waved back, and walked over.
"Jack" he said, holding out his hand. I shook it. "Glad I caught you"

"You have news?"

"I do, I was going to call you later, and there's a letter in the post already. You have ten minutes?"

I looked at the ladies "We'll wander around, you go" Chrissy said.

"In that case, yes, I do"

"Excellent, my office?" I nodded, and followed him inside, and to his office.

"Have a seat Jack" he said, closing the door behind me. "Can I get you a drink?"

"No thank you, I've had my fill this morning"

"Right you are" he sat "Well, it's all fairly self-explanatory I suppose. The two girls in question were suspended from close of play Monday, as you've probably been told."

"Elsie mentioned they weren't in, so I drew my own conclusions"

"Quite so. The parents were involved, and they are deeply ashamed of what has happened. They specifically wanted you to know that"

"Thank you"

"Hmm, yes, this is the part where it gets difficult I'm afraid."

"Oh?"

"The local education authority has agreed that they can be expelled from the school"

"That's good though isn't it?" I said.

"Yes, it is. There is a catch though"

"There is?"

"There is." he sighed deeply "I'm afraid they're insisting they can't be expelled until the end of the school year. They said its too close for them to start somewhere else"

"Ah. I see. That's not good"

"No, its not. And, I can only apologise"

"Not your fault sir" I said.

"I have moved them into the other class, but can't guarantee they won't see each other in the playground. I have briefed the staff to monitor and ensure Elsie is ok"
"Thank you headmaster, I really appreciate that"
"Least I could do Jack, wish we could have done more"
"I'll talk to Elsie, I'm sure she'll be ok"
"I hope so, she's a bright child Jack, takes after her father"
I laughed "Thank you sir"
"Anytime Jack, if there's anything else I can do for you, please call me directly" he scribbled his mobile number on a bit of paper and handed it to me.
"Thank you" I said, standing.
He rose, and shook my hand "I'm sorry this happened Jack, and I hope Elsie will be ok. If she isn't, please call me"
"I will headmaster, thank you" I turned, and walked out to try find Chrissy and Fleur. Not great, but a result of sorts. How would Elsie react? I hope they really do look after her in the playground. I'm sure they would, but would be worried anyway. Wasn't looking forward to telling her.
I was still busily trying to figure out how I was going to break the news to Elsie, when Chrissy broke my thought train.
"Hey, what did he want? Was it about the bullying?"
"Yeah it was" I replied "It's not the greatest news, but also not the worst"
"What? Have they been expelled?"
"Erm, yes and no"
"Ok…."
"Gimme a sec to get it right in my head" I took a moment to think, my mind was all over the place. "The two girls will be expelled, but not until the end of term. The LEA has determined that it is too close to the end of term for them to start elsewhere"
"What? Fuck that, that's their problem surely?" Chrissy said, her voice raised

"Hey, hey, calm down" I said, looking around "They've been put into the other class, so she won't be in the same room as them, and she'll be monitored during break times"
"Other class?"
"Yes, there's two classes of Elsie's year"
"Ah, ok. Poor girl, she'll have to put up with it till the end of term"
"I know. The headmaster was very apologetic, out of his control"
"Fuck sake" she said in frustration.
Fleur remained silent, I guess she wasn't keen on getting involved in a sensitive issue.
"Don't know about you two, but I need coffee" she offered in an attempt to break the tension.
"I know just the place" I smiled.
"He'd better have bloody pastries or there'll be trouble" Chrissy said, getting in the car.
We drove home, and walked to the café in near silence. Fleur and I chatted about the village whilst we walked. She really like it. "So much quieter than the big city. You're lucky."
"Yeah, I am" I smiled. I loved this place; small, quiet, yet had everything and everyone I needed.

Tinkle

"Morning fuckw…." Steve was cut off by Chrissy.
"Never mind that, you'd better have pastries" she said.
"Holy fuck. Morning to you too Lenoir" Steve said dumbfounded.
"Well?"
"For my favourite customer? Always" He smiled.
"Thank god. Morning Stephen"
"Favourite customer?" I said, holding my hand up.

"You?" he laughed "You're a fucking piss-taker, not a customer"
"Charming"
"Who's that?" he asked, pointing at Fleur.
"Fleur Lenoir" she said, stepping forward.
"There's more than one?" He said, looking at Chrissy.
"It would appear so" Fleur answered.
"Well, nice to meet you Lenoir two, what can I get you?"
"Ooh, I could kill for a decent cappuccino"
"I think I can sort that" he smiled "You two, usual?"
We nodded. "Ok, please go and sit, I will bring your order to you"
"The fuck?" Chrissy said "You feeling ok?"
"I am fine thank you Christelle" he said.
"Christelle? Wow. Ok…" we want off to find a table away from the madman.
"What's wrong with him today?" Chrissy asked as we sat down.
"He's trying to impress your sister" I said, winking.
"But Willow…" she started.
"No, not in that way, he's just trying to give a good impression"
"Ah, I see. Wow, he obviously doesn't know you" Chrissy said to Fleur.
"What you trying to say?"
"You have a potty mouth"
"That's not true. Is it?" she said, looking at me for help.
"Don't look at me. You do swear a lot though" I said.
"I do not" she insisted.
"Erm, yeah, you do. Always have" Chrissy said.
"Fucking hell" she laughed.
"See!"
"See what?" Steve said, walking up with a tray full of stuff.
"We have the female version of you sat here" Chrissy said, pointing at Fleur.

"Eh? Suave, sophisticated, successful?" Steve said.
"Erm, no. She swears like a trooper" I said.
"Hey! I'm all those things!" Fleur protested.
"So am I" Steve added, paused, then "Wait. Yeah. Ok, I do swear a lot"
"A lot?" Chrissy laughed, mouthful of pastry.
"Ok, ok. A lot a lot" he admitted "Fucking hell, this a witch hunt or something?"
"Yeah, what the fuck guys?" Fleur added, laughing.
"I'm not going to stand here and be insulted by you bunch of dick-wads" Steve said, and stormed off.
"I like him" Fleur said, watching him go.
"He's *very* taken" Chrissy warned.
"Understood little sister, understood" she said, holding her hands up in defence. "He's nice. Not in that kind of way, just in general"
"Hmmm" I said "You ladies have plans for the day?"
"Well, I gotta get to my hotel and check in, so gotta leave at some point"
"You know its not a problem for you to stay at ours?" I said.
"Just weekends really" Chrissy added.
Then, I had a sudden surge of neurological activity: "You can sleep in my office at the weekends"
"What?" Fleur said.
"It has a bathroom, small kitchen. I wand put a bed in there so you can sleep there if you like?"
"That sounds like I'm putting you out" she said.
"Nah, we'll stop in on the way home, see what you think"
"It would be easier" Chrissy added "I guess money isn't an object, but convenience wise, we can have a few drinks without having to worry about you having to get to the hotel"
Fleur thought for a moment. "Hmm… Ok, let's go see it. If you're sure"

"Hey, it'll be like a fold up bed or something, nothing fancy, but it would do wouldn't it?"
"Absolutely" Fleur agreed.
We chatted some more whilst we ate and drank, it was a great morning, and I was more than happy to have met some of Chrissy's family. She didn't have much family, and Fleur should be in the US. The fact that she's here had a great impact on Chrissy. She was over the moon, having her sister back. It must be lonely having no family around.

Hey, tangent!

I know how that feels! I live in Plymstock, and my family live in Holland, and Merseyside. Ok, so my parents moved back to the UK a few years back, but for almost 25 years, I had nobody. Hmm. Sounds great? Nah, its not. I miss my family. A lot. Especially hard when the divorce hit as I had nobody around. It was tough. Friends are great, but no substitute for family.
Not only did I miss my parents and siblings, but also missed my nephews growing up. And vice versa; they missed my kids growing up.

We left the café and stopped in at the office.
"Wow, nice place" Fleur said, walking around
"Thanks. I was thinking of maybe having a bed here?" I said, indicating an area behind Kyle's desk, separated from view with an office divider screen.
"Perfect" she said "Works for me"
"Excellent. I'll order the bed today, should be here Monday or so I guess. You ok with the hotel just for this weekend?"
"Yes, of course, no problem. Give you guys a bit of p&q"
"Settled then" I said, smiling. I had a good idea! *Wow, bout time you did!* Hey!

Fleur went straight off and packed up her stuff when we got back to the house. Ten minutes later, she was ready to go "Right you guys, I'm off. Thank you for your generous hospitality"
"Not a problem" I said "It's nice having you around"
"Ditto" Chrissy said, hugging her sister.
"Thanks. Hopefully not for too long. See you guys Monday?"
"Monday?" Chrissy said.
"Yeah, I might have some time to myself if that's ok. Might fit in a day in London too. You guys have a good weekend, don't worry about me"
"You sure?" I asked.
"Yep, all good"
"You be careful, and take care" Chrissy said, hugging her again
"See you Monday"
"Thanks again guys, see ya"
And with that, she was gone. She closed the front door behind her, leaving us in silence. It was saddening. The house felt empty. Chrissy must have thought the same "Wow. Silence" she said.
"Yeah, depressing isn't it?"
"Take me out for a walk"
"Nature reserve?" I suggested.
"Great idea"
"Ok, but don't push me in the lake again"
"Deal" she laughed.
A few minutes later, we were in the car, on our way to Holme Fen. The weather was perfect, and I was looking forward to a nice walk around the woods with my girlfriend. *Girlfriend, lol.* Shut up.

It was absolutely beautiful; the sun was filtering through the trees, the birds were singing, I had a beautiful woman on my arm. What else could I possibly need? *A shag?* Shush!
"What's he saying?" Chrissy asked, as we walked.

"What?"

"Inner voice. You have that distant look when you're doing the whole inner monologue thing"

"I do?" *We do?*

"You do."

"Oh. I was just thinking about Elsie" *No you weren't!* Shush.

"Yeah, that's going to be a tough one. How long till the end of term?"

"20 July, just under a month"

"Let's hope the school are true to their word and look after her"

"I hope so"

"You sure that's all that's going on?"

"What?" *She knows!* Knows what? *Everything.* Go away.

"You sure there's nothing else bothering her?"

"I don't know" I didn't. What else could she mean?

"You think maybe the divorce or separation is affecting her?"

"I've talked to her about it, and she seemed ok"

"You think maybe someone impartial talking to her might help?"

"Like?"

"So I know I mentioned James talking to Katy in work, remember her?"

"Yes"

"I dropped the ball on that one, so called her yesterday, she's free Monday between 10 and 12, and can see both of them if you want"

"She would?"

"Yes, up to you though"

"The kids have school, so they won't be available, unless I take them out"

"Your call, she's only free Monday though"

"Let me talk to the kids later"

"Ok, cool"

She took my hand, and walked on through the trees, birch trees with awesome white bark. It was quiet; only the sounds of nature were audible. No humans. No dogs. Just birds. Ducks, geese, herons, various others. No a bird spotter, but it was nice to see a variety of birds at the lake.

I was enjoying the nature all around, and the company I had. Every now and then the scent of her perfume filled my senses; it was just perfect. What a woman.

Her proposal was playing on my mind. Did I want the kids speaking to what was effectively a counselor? *Helped you though right?*
True, but did I want that for my kids?
You don't think they need it?
Dunno. Doubts.
I do.
You do?
Yes. They just have you and that other fucker to talk to.
Other fucker? Helen?
Yeah, that one.
Ok.
Think about it; you think they're going to open up to you? Or her?
Probably, at least, I'd like to hope they would.
They're far too scared of hurting you. A stranger is different.
Hmm. I suppose.
Just try it?
Ok, I will. Thanks.
Welcome innit.
I'd talk to the kids about it later, and call the school, telling them they have a medical appointment.
Good plan.

"You ok there? At it again?"
I shook out of my funk. "Yeah, just thinking about the kids"

"And?"
"I think it's a good idea, and I'll talk to them later"
"Yeah, you said that just now"
"Fuck. Of course I did. I'll let the school know that they have a medical appointment"
She hugged me "You won't regret it, they need someone to talk to"
"I know. I know"
She was right; I wouldn't regret it. It was a good move, and I found out a lot more about my children as a result.
"You gong to tell Helen?" she asked
"What? No, not really. Why? You think I should?"
"Up to you, whatever you think"
"You got me thinking now. No. Fuck her. She doesn't need to know"
"Ok, whatever you think is best"
My stomach rumbled. *Time to eat!* Yeah, good plan.
"What is?" she asked
"Huh?"
"A good plan?"
"Oh, erm, lunch?"
"That *is* a good plan"
We walked back towards the car park, which was empty, save for our car.
"Hey, come here" Chrissy said, running behind a tree.
"What?"
"Come here"
I walked over.
"Kiss me"
She pulled me towards her, and we locked lips. We were like a pair of teenagers, hiding in the woods, making out.
"I love you so much" she said in a husky voice, coming up for air.
"I love you too"

We went at it again. I wanted her so much, and I got the impression the feeling was mutual. Her hands started wandering. Oh my god yes! It's going to happen! Here, in the woods! Fuck yeah!

And you know what? It probably would have. If her phone hadn't started ringing...

"Fuck" she said, disappointed "Who's that?"

She reluctantly let go, and pulled her phone out. "Oh shit, I need to take this" She walked back onto the path and started talking to whomever it was. I took a moment to compose myself, then followed her.

She was stood, leaning against the car. "Yes, of course I can. I'm not home at the moment, but will be back in half an hour or so. I'll send it straight away"

Work.

I sat in the car, and waited. A minute or so later, the driver's door opened and she plonked down in the seat. "Hey, I got to get home to do some work stuff, sorry"

"Not a problem, we were going home anyways right?"

"Yeah, guess so"

"Not a problem then. Drive on Madame"

Chrissy disappeared straight upstairs when we got in. Whatever it was, it was urgent. I made us both some lunch; just a sandwich and a bit of salad. I took hers up, she was busy on the phone, so I put it on the desk and left her to it. I had mine out in the garden. The cat sauntered over, attracted by the smell of ham. Crafty sod, only shows an interest when there's food to be had. I took a bit of ham out of my sandwich and gave it to her. She gobbled it up and stared at me for more. "No way, go eat your own food". Seeing that there was nothing else coming her way, she disappeared back into the murky depths of the garden to find a shaded area to sleep.

I finished my lunch, and did a cupboard and fridge check. Fuck. I needed to go shopping. I could go now, or wait till the kids get here. I'll wait. They'll enjoy a trip to the supermarket.

It would have been a good time to propose.
What?
Earlier, by the tree.
Probably, yes. But I wanted to do it in Italy, not in dreary old England.
Whatever. Just saying.
Appreciate it.
He/I was right; it would have been a good time to drop onto one knee and ask for her hand in marriage. But, I had to do something before I could do that, and it involved Fleur. Not Chrissy.
Whoa! Steady on!
Not that you muppet. Something else. Completely innocent, by the way. I just needed a chat.
Boring.
I checked upstairs; Chrissy was still busy on the phone. I pulled out my mobile, and dialed Fleur's number.
"Hi Jack, what's up"
"Hey, erm, I have a question to ask if that's ok?"
"Sure, shoot"
"I'm going to propose to your sister"
"Oh my god!" she yelled down the phone "That's so amazing! Does she know?"
"No, of course not."
"Oh my god, a surprise. She'll love it!"
"I hope so. Anyways, I wanted to ask your Mother's permission. Can you take me to the cemetery?
"You sure? That sounds terribly old fashioned"
"I'm an old fashioned kind of guy. It feels wrong doing it without asking"

"Ok, no problem. When?"
"Sunday morning?"
"Ok, no problem. I'm in London all day Saturday so it works out"
"Excellent. Is nine o'clock ok? I want to do it early"
"Yeah, that's fine by me. You want me to pick you up from the café?"
"Yes please"
"Ok, see you at nine"
"Thanks Fleur"
"No worries"
I dialed off. Wow. I was nervous already. *Why though? Not like she's going to answer.* I know that you idiot, just nervous anyway. *Melt.*

Tangent.

Seems weird? Why not ask her dad? Her dad left them. *They died together though?* Re-phrase; he *was* leaving them. They had decided to split up a few days before the crash. The night out was something they had arranged with friends, and didn't want anyone to know they were splitting up, so they went. Together. And died. Together. Chrissy had never forgiven her father. It had been at his insistence that they had gone to the theatre. Her mother hadn't wanted to go. Kind of explained why she didn't visit their graves. I wasn't going so I could ask him though I respected her feelings and asked her mother. (For clarity; this is one of those things that didn't happen to me. It was someone I know. And it was the girl's father he asked, as her mother still lives)

"Ugh. Thank you for lunch" she said, walking out onto the patio.
"Welcome. Last minute work emergency?"

"Hmm. I have to give evidence in court"
"Wow, when?"
"Oh, not till next month, but not something I like doing"
"I can imagine"
"I'll have to go down to London and stay overnight though…" she added with cheeky smile.
"Oh, how nice for you. More reading?"
"You're coming with me, idiot" Shoulder punch.
I laughed "I look forward to it"
"Me too, maybe we'll be able to fit something in"
"Like a show or something?"
"Or something. How about a play at the Globe?" she suggested.
"Sounds good to me, I'll look into it"
"Brilliant" she dropped back into her chair and relaxed.
"We'll need to go shopping later"
"Later. First we chill"
"Good idea" I closed my eyes and allowed myself to drift off.
Ok, so I hadn't planned on sleeping too long, but it didn't work. I was out. So was Chrissy.
We were rudely awoken when Elsie came running in and jumped on me "Daddy!"
Whoa! What the fuck? "Hello angel" I said, with a big smile. I hugged my little girl I missed you"
"I missed you too"
She jumped down and repeated the process with Chrissy.
James was obviously far more reserved, I got up and gave him a quick hug. "Good to see you buddy"
"You too dad" he smiled "You didn't forget the footie tomorrow right?"
"Of course not. Looking forward to it" There was an obvious sigh of relief from James, almost like he didn't trust me to remember. Little sod.
"Go sort yourselves out, we've got to go shopping whenever you're ready" I said.

They both trudged off upstairs to do whatever. Texting probably. My kids are here! I laughed to myself.
"You ok?" Chrissy asked.
"Super happy" I said, contentedly.
"I can tell, good to see"
I was happy. I had missed my kids like crazy. But, they were home. *They've only been gone a few hours*. Doesn't matter. Doesn't matter at all. *Good to see you happy man*. Ta.

Stomping on the stairs indicated readiness. "Let's go" I said to Chrissy, and very reluctantly, we got up. Shopping was great; we didn't run into anybody, and the kids did their usual of chucking random shite in the trolley.
I didn't mind; I liked buying them stuff. We had pizza for dinner, those nice fresh made ones they do at supermarkets. It was lively with discussion and random chatter. I loved every second of it.
We did our usual Friday thing of slouching and watching a movie after dinner. Lego Batman. Love it. *That's a usual Friday night thing?* No, but I like the idea of it. *Fair*.
After dinner, the kids went off to do whatever kids do, I'm guessing Gaming for James, and Texting for Elsie.
Chrissy and I went for a couple of beers in the Beer Garden, listened to music, and played 007 Trivial Pursuit. It was a great ending to a so-so day.

In bed, I reflected on what had been a weird day. I had a check list to go through tomorrow:
1. Speak to Elsie
2. Go to football
3. Ask Helen about her situation. (Just an update, not that I cared)
4. Speak to both kids about seeing Katy

Wasn't looking forward to some of those. Though, the football should take my mind off things.

Tomorrow was going to be a great day. I'd been looking forward to it for a while. I know James had too. Hopefully my boy and his team would kick some ass.

In the meantime...

I put my headphones in, and had to run to Paddington station in order to catch Holmes and Watson on the outbound Dover train. I made it. Just.

Day 14, Saturday, 23rd of June.

Wake up!
What?
Wake up you melt! This is it!
Eh? I opened my eyes. The world came into focus slowly. Correction; Chrissy came into focus slowly.
She was lying on her side, leaning on her elbow. "Morning handsome" she smiled.
"Morning" I said.
LOOK DOWN YOU ABSOLUTE FUCKING MUPPET!
My eyes obeyed. "Oh. Hello" I said. She was naked. Or just topless? I didn't know. *We don't give a fuck either way, get in there sunshine! Motorboat those puppies!* What?
"You see something you like?" she said, purposely wiggling her chest.
"Erm. Yeah, I do actually" *Is that the best you can do? Fuck me...*
Now, as you probably know, Sod's law dictates that bad shit usually happens at the worst possible time. It did. Just as I was about to get a feel/taste of heaven, the door opened. Chrissy instinctively pulled up the duvet, just managing to cover her modesty before Elsie ran in and jumped on the bed.
"Can we have pancakes please Daddy?" she beamed, totally oblivious to what she had interrupted. *What the actual fuck?? Pancakes?? Baps!* Calm down.
"Of course my angel" I said, and kissed her head. "Did you sleep ok?"
"Yes thank you"
"Good. Shall we all get up together?" I said turning to Chrissy.
"I'll be down in a minute" she said.
"Come on, let's all go together" I said.
"Yeay!" Elsie said.

Chrissy fixed me with a stare, her eyes stabbing me multiple times with tiny daggers.
I laughed. "Maybe we'll go, and give Chrissy a moment" I said, getting up, and following Elsie out of the room.
I looked back before I left, and Chrissy pulled down the duvet, exposing herself. She winked and said "Yeah, see you in a minute Beckett"
What a woman. Oh!

Elsie helped me put together a breakfast worthy of a champion, ready for when James came down. And he did, just after we'd finished.
"Wow, breakfast looks good" he smiled.
"I helped, we did it for you, to make you strong for the football" Elsie said proudly.
He hugged her "Thanks squidge, it looks great"
"Morning champ" I chimed in.
"Morning dad. Thanks" He smiled. He looked happy. Very happy. Unusually happy. Suspiciously happy.
"You ok?" I asked.
"Yep" he said, sitting down, and helping himself to the stack of pancakes.
"Ok…" I made myself a coffee, and heard Chrissy come down. I turned "You want a cofffff….." The word died in my mouth. My brain helpfully replaced it with: "Whoa!" *Holy fuck!*
"Coffee? Yes please" she said smiling. *Dude!* Yes, I can see thanks. *Fit as fuck!*
"You look nice" I said, hoping inner voice's last comment hadn't come out. I looked at James, who was smiling like a Cheshire cat. *No fucking wonder!*
"Thanks, I borrowed a shirt from James, thought I'd show my support" She was wearing one of James' football shirts, which was quite obviously just a tiny bit too small for her, in all the right places, if you know what I mean.

A pair of running shorts and trainers completed the look.
"Yes" I said "I can see that" Wow. *I fucking love this woman.* So do I...

Whatever you're imagining right now is exactly what she looked like. Jesus H Christ… There were going to be a lot of happy teenage boys at the tournament today.

Tangent?

"What the fuck are you talking about, you idiot?"
Ok. I know the guys out there will back me up: There's just something about a woman in a football shirt. Especially if it's your team's shirt. Trust me ladies; it's a thing.
Imagine, if you will, a woman, just clothed in an LFC shirt, she turns, and it says Fowler on the back. Holy shit batman! Jackpot!
For clarity; this would usually not involve underwear of any kind.
Fortunately, in this case, there was a bra. And I'm guessing pants. Hopefully.
To try this at home, simply substitute her pyjamas for a football shirt… she'll roll her eyes, but will do it for you anyway. Result!
Anyway…

In shock, I turned back and made another coffee.
"You all ready for today?" she asked James.
"Oh yes, today is going to be a great day" he beamed. I wasn't sure if he was talking about the football, or the kudos he was going to get from his mates…
We finished breakfast, and scattered. I was left with all the dishes, as per usual. Elsie was getting dressed, James was in the shower, and Chrissy was out in the back garden, on the phone to her sister.

Half an hour later, we were in the car, on our way to the tournament. The sun was shining, the mood was superb, and we were looking forward to a great day. The majority of James' team were already there when we drove into the car park. We got out, James got his bag, and trotted over to join his friends. "Good luck James!" Chrissy shouted as he joined them. They all looked over, and the collective jaws dropped. James was instantly bombarded with questions from his mates, who couldn't believe what they'd just seen. She'd transformed him into the most popular guy at the tournament. She knew exactly what she was doing.

What a woman.

"Come on, lets go see where his first match is" I said, pointing at the fixtures board by the clubhouse.

We walked over, and a spark of recognition fired in my brain. A car. Familiar. Oh well…

And it soon became clear what the spark was.

Helen.

Fuck sake.

She was stood by the board, trying to see where she needed to go to watch the first game.

"Shit" I said.

"What?" Chrissy said.

I nodded towards Helen.

"Oh shit" she said.

"Mummy!" Elsie shouted. Shit, this was all I needed.

Helen turned, and saw us. She walked over to meet us.

"Hello my little angel" she said, kneeling, and holding out her arms. Elsie ran into them and hugged her mother.

After, she stood. "Hello Jack"

"Helen" I said simply.

"Hello…Chrissy wasn't it?" she said, looking Chrissy up and down.

She turned to me "Strange, I didn't know you were into that kind of thing Jack"
"Oh you'd be surprised" Chrissy said. I elbowed her in the ribs.
"What? Just saying"
"Yeah, thanks" I said. *Uh-oh, this is awkward...*
Helen was dressed in jeans, converse, and a hoodie. Not in a million years could I imagine her turning up in what Chrissy was wearing. Score one for Lenoir!
Helen took a breath. "Anyway, I was hoping to have seen James before his game" she said, still looking at Chrissy's outfit.
"He's gone off to get ready, his mates were happy to see him this morning" I said.
"Yes, I can imagine" Still staring. Eventually, she was able to divert her gaze, and lower herself to looking at me instead. "Is he ok?"
"Yeah, he's totally great actually" I said.
"Right" she said "We're going to be here all morning. Can we please try not to turn it into a point scoring contest?" she said, looking at Chrissy again.
Wait, was she implying that we were going to hang around together all morning? That wasn't on my agenda... I looked at Chrissy, she just smiled. She was on a cloud of her own today. She simply took Elsie's hand, saying "Come on Ello, let's go find your bro"
They walked off, leaving me with her. Fuck sake. Thanks Chrissy.
What the fuck was I meant to do now? Jesus.

"Morning fuckbag"
Thank fuck. Steve.
I turned, and saw Steve walking over with Willow. I had never been so happy to see him.
"Hey mate" I said with a massive smile. He walked up and gave me a massive bear hug.

"You ok man?" he asked, knowing full well that Helen could hear.

"Yeah, I'm good"

"Excellent. Where are my two little monsters?" he said whilst I hugged Willow.

"James is with his team, Ello is over there with Chrissy" I said, pointing.

He looked over to where Chrissy was standing with Elsie.

"Holy shit. Is she wearing a footie shirt?" he said.

Willow elbowed him in the ribs. "Easy tiger"

"Hi Steve" Helen said, trying to fit in with the group.

"Oh, hi Helen" he said, and carried on ignoring her.

It was silent for a moment, then she said. "Is this your girlfriend? How far along is she? Congratulations"

"This is Willow" he said half-heartedly.

Helen held out her hand to Willow "I'm Helen"

"Yes, I know" Willow said, weakly shaking her hand.

This was awkward as fuck. I was kind of hoping that Helen would fuck off and stand somewhere away from us, but I got the impression she wasn't going to. But then…

"Well, I'm going to go get a cup of tea, can I get anyone anything?" Helen asked.

A resounding negative response from all told her all she needed to know. "Right, I'll go get one for myself then" she said awkwardly and walked off.

"What the fuck is she doing here?" Steve asked when she was out of earshot.

"Supporting her son?" I offered.

"Fuck right off, since when has she been interested in his football?" he said.

I shrugged "Fuck knows, it's awkward as fuck. You should have seen the look she gave Chrissy"

"I can imagine" he said.

"Shall we go join them?" Willow said, nodding towards where Chrissy and Ello were.
"Yeah, come on"
"Yeah, fuck her" Steve added. Fuck her indeed. *What?* Not literally you knob, as in she can fuck right off? *Ah, gotcha.*
We walked over to the pitch where James was to play his first game. Chrissy and Ello had secured us a spot by the centre line. Not that it was difficult; there weren't like thousands of people there. Small groups of proud families were dotted around the pitch. I recognised a lot of the parents, but, as per usual, I got ignored. Helen, on the other had, was busy doing the rounds of the various groups, cup of tea in hand. Chatting away, smiling, laughing. I fucking hated her. She'd managed to alienate me from these people, and for what? Because we split up?
No doubt they all thought it was my fault, and that Chrissy was the cause.
"Fuck them all mate" Steve said, reading my mind. "You don't need them"
"I know. Still hurts though"
"Ach, fuck them, and fuck her" he replied.
"Yeah, you're right" I snapped out of it, and concentrated on the game. The teams were on the pitch, and James gave us a quick wave.
"He seems popular today" Steve said "Wonder why?"
Willow rolled her eyes "Jesus, it's just a football shirt" she said.
"Yeah Steve" I added. But gave him a look that said I totally agreed with him. (squint eyes, nod slowly)
Willow shook her head "Men"
Fortunately, Helen chose to stand with a group on the opposite side of the pitch.

The game kicked off, and it was obvious from the outset that James' team were all over the opposition in the first half.

Chrissy shouted encouragement throughout, and got encouraging looks from all the dads, accompanied by head shaking from the mums.

At half time, Steve said "Why don't we go get some drinks and snacks mate" He winked theatrically.

"Yeah, ok" I said, playing along with whatever was going on.

We walked over to the clubhouse "What's the script?" I asked.

"Pint innit" he smiled. "I'm not driving son"

Smiling, we walked into the clubhouse, which was already full of happy dads. We made our way through the crowd to the bar and ordered two pints of their finest bitter.

"Cheers" he said.

"Cheers mate. Thank fuck you came"

"I'll drink to that. Let's just hope that fucker doesn't turn up in the bar eh"

"Amen" I said, holding up my glass in salute.

"Must have been awkward" he said. I knew what he meant.

"Yeah, it was. I can't believe she's here. She normally doesn't bother. And she made a real thing of Chrissy's outfit"

"Not being funny mate, but I would as well. Jesus. You scored a good one there sunshine. And fuck her anyway. Don't let her get to you. I've seen here with all those other ignorant fuckers. Screw the lot of them"

He was right of course. Fuck them all. Dickheads.

We finished our pints and got some cans and choccy bars for the girls.

"Oh shit" I said as we walked back

He looked over "Of for fuck sake! Can't she just fuck off?"

Helen was stood with the girls, trying to engage them in conversation. They looked unhappy about her being there.

"Hey guys" I said as we got there "Got some drinks, and bars of choc"

I handed the loot to Chrissy, and motioned to Helen to follow me.

We walked away from the group.

"What's up?" she asked.

"Look Helen, I get that you're here to support James, for the first time ever."

"Thanks for that" she said.

"Look, I don't think you hanging out with us is a great idea, do you?"

"What do you mean?" She asked.

"Oh come on Helen, for fuck sake. What are you dong here? Are you just trying to make things awkward for me?"

"I'm here to support my son" she said defiantly.

I laughed "Don't give me that shit. Why don't you go do that with some of your friends" I said.

"Our friends Jack" she corrected.

I laughed "Fuck sake. Are you for real? Not one of those bastards has given me the time of day since you upped and left me. You're welcome to them though"

"That's not true" she said looking puzzled "Is it?"

"Of course it is. I've been blanked by everyone we know, here and at the school. It's like they all think I'm some sort of heartless fucker that walked out on his family"

"Well, if that's what they think, I don't know where they get the idea from" she said, flustered.

"Yeah, ok. I wonder. Anyway, it's probably best if you go hang out with them rather than making our day uncomfortable"

"Since when do I make you uncomfortable?" she asked.

I could feel the rage building inside me. "Since you fucking left me and destroyed our family?" I said angrily. People turned their heads, and looked at us.

"Jesus Jack, no need for that" she said, all flustered.

"Every need for that. Sorry if the truth hurts" I said, and walked back to my love, my kids, my friends, my only family. *Fuck yeah, you tell the bitch!*

I mentally high-fived my inner voice, leaving Helen standing, all eyes on her. Embarrassed, she hurried off, to get as far away from us as possible.

Have a taste of your own medicine. Fucker.

Meanwhile, the second half was about to kick off. James played his heart out, I felt so proud of him. He had a great group of friends, and… And? Where is his girlfriend? *Oh shit.* I hoped they hadn't broken up. *Maybe she had something else on?* Who knows. *He didn't seem upset, so maybe that was it.* Let's hope so. They won the game 2-0, and progressed to the next round.

We didn't see Helen for the rest of the tournament; she didn't even come to find James at the end to congratulate him. Maybe she'd left after I'd had a go at her. Good. *Serves her fucking right.* In the end, it was a long day; James' team made it to the final, but sadly lost. Second place was a fucking great effort. My heart swelled with pride. At the end, all of his team came over to say hi, and to thank Chrissy for her fantastic support. Boys eh, brave in a group… She was extremely gracious, and high-fived them all with a big smile. Not as big as the smiles on their faces as they walked away though…

"Hey buddy" Steve said, grabbing hold of James "Great effort man, proud of you"

"Thanks Uncle Steve" he said, smiling.

"How about pizza, on me?"

Nobody argued, and we drove on to Huntingdon for pizza. Despite the whole saga with Helen, it was actually a great day.

Tangent.

So, I got the chance to actually go to Ramsey Forty Foot last week (5 Aug 24), as I was in the area. Looks nothing like it does in my mind/books. That's not a slight on the village, but just the reality.

My village is more old fashioned, narrow roads, thatched roofs, etc. Ramsey itself also looks nothing like what I had in mind. It actually looks more like my idea of Ramsey Forty Foot…
Random, I know, just thought I'd share that with you.

After we'd had pizza, we invited Steve and Willow back to ours. They wanted to go home first, but said they'd only be an hour or so. Suited us; James needed to shower etc, and I wanted a nap.
WUT?
Dude. I'm tired.
Tired? What the fuck is wrong with you? You old prick.
Beer in the afternoon makes me tired.
Eh? Since When?
Since erm, dunno.
Penis.
Fuck you. I'm going anyway.
And I did. I needed like 30 ins or so, and Chrissy said she'd just busy herself with putting a wash on, and getting the garden ready for the visitors. Suited me. I racked out.
Punctual to the second, 30 minutes later, Chrissy punched my shoulder "Wake up you lazy sod"
"Ouch. Wow, any need?" I said groggily, rubbing my shoulder.
"They'll be here in a sec, sort yourself out"
"Yeah, ok, gimme a minute or so"
I got up, ran my head under a cold tap in the bathroom, and was ready to go again.

Minor tangent.

I'm not the only one right? Having beer in the afternoon fucks you up. I'm always tired as hell after.
Please say its not just me eh?

Our guests didn't turn up for another 30 minutes; apparently, Steve had fallen asleep on the sofa as soon as they'd gotten home. See, not just me.

We sat out in the garden, where the sun was still shining nicely. It was getting close to five in the evening, but nobody was hungry thankfully. I really couldn't be arsed to cook. We'd put some nibbles and stuff out, which seemed to be enough.

"Here, you look like you fucking need this" Steve said, handing me a cold beer.

"Cheers bud"

"You been ok?"

"As in...?"

"You know, that blood pressure bollocks"

"Ah, yeah, getting better actually. Bp is getting back to normal"

"Hey, that's great news" he said, smiling

"It sure is. Not sure Helen helped today though"

His smile disappeared instantly. "Nah, that fucker always seems to turn up where she's not wanted"

"She does, doesn't she?"

"What did you say to here to make here storm off like that?"

"Ach, mate, she was going on about shit, and I told he to stand with her friends instead of us. She said they were our friends, and I put her straight on that. I told her she was making us all feel uncomfortable."

"Fucking right she was"

"Yeah right. So, then she asked since when did she make me feel uncomfortable"

"And?"

"I shouted at her. Basically since you left me and fucked up our family"

"Good fucking effort mate" he said, and we high-fived.

"What's going on here?" Chrissy asked "Looks awfully suspicious?"

"Guy stuff" I winked.

"Fucking guy stuff?" she said, laughing.
"Hey" Steve said "We have stuff as well you know"
"Yeah, I'm sure you do" Willow laughed.
"Feels like these two are taking the piss mate" he said to me
"How about we just go somewhere else?" I suggested.
"You can fuck right off" Chrissy said "You're not going to the friggin pub"
"Us?" Steve said, looking innocently at both ladies.
"No way Fletch" Willow said, wagging her finger at him.
"Fuck" he said, hanging his head.
"You have a pub right there" Chrissy said, nodding towards the bar.
Steve looked over at the pub "Hey, it's the Garden Bar now? Since when?"
"My idea" Chrissy said proudly. "And I had a sign made up"
We all looked at the sign, which she'd put up whilst I'd been having my nap.
"The Garden Bar?" I said.
"What? You don't like?" she shot me a look that said I'd better…
"No, not at all. I mean, of course I do. Ach fuck, you know what I mean" I was confusing myself.
She laughed "I think so"
Willow supported her friend "I think it's lovely, and very apt; you like gardening, and he likes pub"
"I love pub" I blurted.
"Yeah, me to" Steve said, but still gave me a puzzled look. I just shrugged. *Where the fuck did that come from?*
The pub sign had a pint of beer with a climbing rose wrapped around it, with a rake and shovel crossed over each other behind it.. I loved it.

The deal was struck; we spent the rest of the evening/night in the Garden Bar.

The drinks were free, and the company was great.
The kids? James was knackered, so spent his time playing on his playstation, then bed. Ello had a bath, did her nails, and chatted to her mates. Followed by bed.
Any more questions?
Come to mention it….
Go on then.

1. Does your mum still text you every day to check up on you?

Answer: Not everyday any more since I was with Chrissy. She trusted me to be ok as I wasn't on my own. Still asked once a week or so though.

2. Pam? Still see her? Not mentioned a lot in this book.

Answer: Yeah, once a fortnight on average. I didn't want to harper on about it all the time. Just accept it as a part of my life.

3. Erm. Can't think of anything else.

Ok, let me know if you have more questions ok? Anytime.
Can we get back to the story now?
You think you've had enough of a break to think of something to write? Got a bit stuck did we? Resorting to reader's questions! Dick.
Fuck you.

Anyhow, regardless of that bullshit…
We all had a fantastic time. Steve more so than anyone else, poor Willow had to support the bugger all the way home. Fortunately, I didn't have that problem; my bed was upstairs.

I lay in bed trying to focus on the days events, but the fucking room was spinning to fast.

I fell out of bed, ran-crawled to the bog, and threw up.
After I'd swilled my mouth out with mouthwash, I stumbled back to bed.
Chrissy just looked at me shaking her head "Pathetic"
I fell on the bed and zonked out immediately. Fuck the headphones.

Day 15, Sunday, 24th of June.

I'd like to say I slept right through the night, but that would be a lie. I was up several times throughout the night to empty my aching bladder, and to drink precious water. My head was splitting, making it even harder to sleep. *You absolute fucking loser.*
Yeah, not going to argue that one.
I was woken by Chrissy shaking me saying I had a phone call. She handed me her phone "Hello?"
"Motherfucker, you'd best get down here straight away"
"Steve?" My head was still foggy.
"Lenoir two is sat here waiting for your pathetic arse"
Lenoir two? Oh fuck. Fleur. Sunday. I looked at the time; it was almost half past nine. "Shit, on way"
I dialled off, and ran into the bathroom. I had a super fast shower, got dressed, and went to head out.
Chrissy was in the kitchen "Where you off to in such a rush?"
"I totally forgot I said I'd help Steve out this morning"
"With what? It's Sunday"
"The thing" I said. *The fucking thing?*
"The thing?"
"Yeah, you know, the thing. Won't be long" I blew her a kiss and left before she could stop me.
I ran to the cafe, and burst in, out of breath, my head absolutely killing me.
"Fucking hell, here it is" Steve said.
"Morning. Sorry I'm late" I looked for Fleur.
"Out in the garden" he said.
"Ta mate" I went to go outside.
"Oi, here, have this first" he handed me a glass of water and two paracetamol. "Get your head straight"

I popped the pills and washed them down with the water
"Cheers bud"
Fleur was sat at one of the tables sipping coffee "Morning" she smiled.
Amazement. She wasn't pissed. "Morning. I'm so sorry I'm late"
"It's cool, gave me time to enjoy this." she said, holding up her cup "You want one?"
"We have time?"
"Yeah, I got fuck all else to do today, other than waiting on your sorry arse that is" she smiled.
"Sorry"
"I'm yanking your chain" she said "Go get a coffee"
"Thanks" I said, and went back inside.
"Still alive then?" Steve commented.
"Yeah, she's super understanding" I said "Can I get a coffee please mate"
"Help your fucking self" he said. And I did; I made myself a flat white, and went back out to sit with Fleur.
"You sure you want to do this thing?" she asked "You know you don't have to right?"
"I know, I just want to do it right" I said.
"Ok, up to you"
"Can I ask you a question?"
"Shoot"
"Why would Chrissy not visit your parents graves?"
"Wow, that's a big one" she said. "You sure you want to know?"
"I think so"
"If I tell you, you have to promise me you'll never tell Christelle"
"Ok…"
"Not joking, deadly serious. Promise"
"I promise" *What, was she like a prostitute or something??*

There was a bit of thinking, a sip of coffee, then she told me why.

"I can't really think of any other way of saying it, other than…"

"Hey, so, what are you guys up to out here?" Steve said, suddenly appearing next to me.

"Fuck me!" I shit myself.

Fleur turned to him and gave him a look that said "Why don't you just fuck off".

He read her mind, and slowly backed away "Ok…."

When he'd gone, she turned to me and carried on "Yeah, so basically, they're not our real parents"

I spat out my coffee. "What?"

"Eww! Gross!" she said, wiping coffee off her hand.

Yeah, like fucking WHAT?

"What? No need to swear" she said, still mopping up coffee from the table. *Keep it inside dude!*

"Apologies. They're not your parents?"

"I thought I said that already?"

"You did, I'm just trying to get my head round what I just heard" I said. What the fuck? Not her parents? *Could be worse mate, at least she wasn't a prostitute.* Watch yourself…

"Around what? We're adopted. I thought that was fairly fucking simple to work out" she said

"Erm, yeah, I guess so. But still."

"So you see, there's no real need for you to ask mum, there's no point really. They told me, and not her. She doesn't know. She doesn't visit them because she fell out with both of them massively over the divorce"

"Wow, why haven't you told her?"

"I didn't want to upset her any more than she already was during the divorce. I was kind of hoping she'd do well at school and go onto uni. Which she did, so I guess it worked out ok"

"Ok for you maybe, not for her"

"You're right. I've just never had the courage to tell her. It's quite a big thing"
"I can see that, but don't you think she deserves to be told now?"
"Well, I guess so. Fuck. Why are you so good at guilt-tripping?"
"It's a gift" I winked.
"Fucking hell" She shook her head in defeat. "Ok, finish your drink, go home, and tell her to come here"
I downed my coffee and ran back home.

When I got there, the kids were sat having a lazy breakfast. There was a stack of pancakes in the middle of the table, and the three of them were busy eating and chatting.
"Sorry to ruin a precious moment" I said , sitting down "But your sister wants to see you at the cafe"
"Fleur? Why? I'm eating"
"Dunno, but I kind of got the impression she meant now…"
"Wow" she said, putting her cutlery down "Like right now?"
I nodded "Like right now"
She sighed, and got up. I slid into her seat, and finished off her pancake.
"This better be good" she said angrily, picking up her phone and handbag.
"Oh, I think it is" I said.
"What?" she turned to me.
"Oh, nothing, go on, best you get going"
She fixed me with a death glare, then turned and left.
"What's going on dad?" James asked.
"Oh, just grown up stuff, boring" I said, and helped myself to more food.

Meanwhile, at the cafe….

Tinkle…

"Morning Lenoir, you ok?"
"I'm tired, and starving"
"I can cure both" Steve winked "Go, she's sat out side"
Chrissy walked out the back, and saw Fleur sitting at the table, playing ith her phone. She was the only person here.
"Moring" Chrissy grunted, sitting down.
"Morning sis" Fleur said "You look like shit"
"Wow, thanks. What is it you want? I was just getting stuck into a stack of pancakes"
"Sorry. You want me to get you something?"
"Its ok, Steve is sorting me out. Why don't you tell me why I'm here"
"Ok, well, there aint no easy way of saying this"
"You're staying for good?"
"What? No. Although, I am tempted" Fleur said.
Steve came out with a tray, and put it on the table for Chrissy.
"Sorted" he said, and went back inside. On the tray was a cappuccino and two cinnamon swirls. What a guy.
Chrissy tucked in, and encouraged Fleur to carry on talking.
"Oh, yes, erm, so yeah, no easy way to say it."
"So you said" Chrissy said with a mouthful of pastry, she took a large swig of coffee.
"Yeah, so, we're adopted"
Chrissy spat out her coffee all over the table
"Fuck sake, not again!" Fleur yelled, coffee dripping from her hands. She picked up a napkin and started cleaning herself up.
"We're fucking what now?" Chrissy said incredulously.
"Adopted"
"Adopted…"
"Yes, that's what I said"
"How the fuck do you know that?"
"They told me"

"Who?"
"Who? The fucking space monkeys. Who do you think?"
"Don't you dare get pissy with me" Chrissy warned.
Fleur held up her hand "Sorry. Look, I should have told you sooner, but could just never work up the courage"
"So you just thought you'd leave it? Thanks a fucking bunch"
Fleur sighed. "I probably never would have told you if it wasn't for Jack"
"You're not making it any better for yourself" Chrissy said angrily.
"Look, I don't give a flying fuck if you're angry with me. You know how difficult a thing that is to tell someone?"
"Yes, I can imagine its a fucking nightmare!" Chrissy yelled. She put her head in her hands, and fell silent.
"I'm so sorry Christelle"
Chrissy started sobbing, her whole body shaking with the ferocity, like a lifetime of pent up emotion flooding out. Fleur moved her chair next to hers, and put her arms around her. Chrissy did the same. The two sisters were in each others arms, both crying. One because she was guilty as sin, the other because her whole world had just fallen apart. They sat like that for a good ten minutes, getting it all out of their system.
Slowly, they sat up in their respective chairs, and composed themselves. Almost simultaneously, they said "You look a mess", causing them both to laugh.
"I don't blame you" Chrissy said after they had fallen silent again "I haven't forgiven you either though"
"I can live with that" Fleur said "I deserve as much"
Silence.
Chrissy started crying again "I don't know who I am" she said.
"Hey! You're Christelle Lenoir, you always have been, and always will be"
"But they're not my parents"

"They're the only parents you've ever known, that should be enough. They loved you more than anything in the world"
More silence.
"I need to go see them" Chrissy said calmly.
"Now?" Fleur asked.
"Now" Chrissy said.
They both finished their drinks, ad Chrissy took the remaining cinnamon swirl to eat on the way.

Steve knew better, and stayed in the kitchen until they had left. As soon as they had gone, he pulled out his phone and called me.
"Hello?"
"Jesus fucking Christ, what the actual fuck is going on?"
"She just found out she's adopted"
"Yeah, I gathered that, Chrissy was quite fucking vocal about it"
"Are they still there?"
"No, they fucked off about two minutes ago"
"You know where they went?"
"Not a fucking scooby"
"Hmm, ok, thanks mate"
"No worries, speak later"

I stared at my phone for a while after Steve had called. Should I call her?
You think she's in the fucking mood?
Nah, probably not.
Best leave them to whatever they're up to.
Yeah, you're right.
Gratitude.

Inner voice was right; it was probably best to just leave them alone for the time being.

Worried, I cleared the table whilst the kids were up getting dressed. I'll take them over to see mum and dad, get out of the house in case they come here.

"Guys! We're going over to see nan and grandad in a sec, get your shoes on"

Shouts of joy from Elsie. A few minutes later, we were walking to mum and dads.

Correction; the kids were running, I was walking, doing my best to keep up with them. They got to the house a minute or so before I did. We had a cup of tea, then all went out for a walk with the dog. I was worried about the other two. I checked my phone a few times along the way; no messages.

I didn't tell mum and dad what was going on, as it wasn't really my business to do so. It was a private matter between Chrissy and Fleur.

By the time we said bye to the parents and got back to the house, Fleurs' car was in the drive.

I took a deep breath and opened the door. "Hello?"

"In here" Chrissy shouted from the living room.

I went in and found both sisters on the sofa with a cup of tea.

"Hey"

"Hey" Fleur said. Chrissy stood up and hugged me tight.

"You ok?" I asked.

"Yeah, think so" she said.

"Where have you been?"

"We went to the cemetery. I had to see them"

"And?"

"And its all ok. I'm still angry with Fleur, but I'll get over it"

I looked at Fleur "Hey, I deserve it" she said.

I agreed. I didn't say as much, but I agreed.

"Are you ok with it?" Chrissy asked me.

"Me? Why wouldn't I be?"

"I don't know. I don't know if it changes things"

"Changes what?"

"Everything" she said.
I looked confused "Why would it?"
"Because I don't know who I am" she said, sounding profoundly sad.
"You're the woman I love" I said. This pushed her over some invisible edge, and she fell into my arms in floods of tears.
"I'll go see if the kids are ok" Fleur said, and went upstairs.
"Hey" I said "This changes nothing"
"Are you sure?"
"Yes, I know exactly who you are, its enough for me"
We sank onto the sofa, and stayed there in silence for a while. I didn't want to say anything, I just wanted to comfort my love. I stroked her hair as she lay in my arms, enjoying the feeling of her body against mine. Her body convulsed occasionally, indicating she was still crying, but it got less and less, until it finally stopped. She sat up.
"I must look a right mess"
Yeah, she did. Typical panda eyes, but she still managed to look sexy with it.
"Sexy?" she said, with a little smile.
"Fuck sake" I said "Sorry" *Lol, muppet.*
"No, its ok. At least I know you still fancy me in this state"
"I'd fancy you in any state" I winked.
She smiled. "Right, I'm going to go upstairs and sort myself out, don't want the kids seeing me like this"
"Ok, no worries. I'll go see what there is for dinner"

I went to the kitchen, and had a look through the fridge and cupboards. There really wasn't much of anything as we would be leaving for Italy tomorrow evening. Which reminded me… Ring. I need to make sure I pack the ring in my carry-on bag.
Oh fuck.
What?
You and packing

Yes?
You're a fucking nightmare when it comes to packing.
What? No I'm not.
Bet you check your effing bag about ten times before you go.
I'm not that bad am I?
Erm, yeah, you are.
Oh… Well. Can't help it.
Anyways, dinner. There's not much here, I can do like fish fingers and chips or something. Actually, that sounds pretty good, haven't had fish fingers for a while. Ello didn't really like fish fingers, so good thing for her I was dropping them back to their grandparents for dinner. At least they would have something decent.
Time check; half past three. Good time to go up in the loft and get the travel bag, maybe do a bit of packing. *Yeah, that sounds like fun…*

Tangent.

I'm a fucking nightmare when it comes to packing. Sweet fucking Jesus. I ALWAYS pack far too much. Don't know why, but I always come back with stuff that hasn't been worn. I really try though, but always fail. I have been getting a lot better over the last few years. *Debatable…* Whatever. I think I have.

Anyways, I got the bag down and spent ten minutes or so chucking stuff into it. Chrissy was sat doing her make-up, and didn't comment. I could tell she was dying to though. I zipped the bag up and set it to one side. Done. Sorted.
Yeah right….
Packing done, I tried to think of a good excuse to get the kids out of school tomorrow. Hmmm.
It needed to be something decent, as I didn't want them phoning Helen to ask just what the fuck was going on.

Fuck it, I'll just call the headmaster first thing and tell him the truth. Probably better than making it up and getting caught out. Sorted. What else did I need to do? I'd already arranged the time off with Kyle, and he was happy.

Oh, shit. That reminded me. Irene. Fuck. She wanted to meet me sometime. I'll have to call Kyle and make sure he arranged the meeting after I got back. The trial was this week, which was lucky as I wasn't here, and Kyle would need help to complete all the work for the week. The name still made me smile. Irene Holmes. Genius. I couldn't wait to meet this girl.

Ok, so that was that sorted. What else? *Erm, take your kids home?* What time is it? *Time to go son.*

Fuck. Already? I instantly felt guilty for not having spent much time with them today. Fuck sake.

"You ok there?" Chrissy asked.

"What?"

"Yuo ok? You look like your talking to yourself"

"I was just thinking that I hadn't spent much time with the kids today. They probably think I'm a terrible father"

"Ach, don't be an idiot. They know you can't spent you every waking moment with them"

"We haven't done much today though"

"Not every day has to be fun packed, or rammed with activity. You're allowed a lazy day Jack"

She's right.

"Of course I'm right. Look, I don't want you getting all upset tonight. You've been doing super well this weekend. Your bp is normal, and you had that massive argument with Helen without fainting. That's progress"

"Fuck. You're right" She was. My bp had slowly gone up to normal levels, and I hadn't fainted for a while. "oddly enough though, I don't feel myself spiralling downwards. I feel bad, but it doesn't feel like its going to make me crash. It feels different. Does that make sense?"

"Perfect" she said, and kissed me.
Oh my god. Was I ok? Had I gone through the shit phase? Was I better? I needed to see Pam, but it would have to wait until we got back. Fuck aye! I'm ok! *Let's hope so eh!*
"I'm proud of you" another kiss "Come on, let's get the kids back, then I can get my packing done"

Tangent.

Ok, so I wasn't ok, I was just better. There would still be lapses, but they would be very few and very far between. I had turned a corner.
I still needed my pills, and still do now, but the crippling depressive crying was almost a thing of the past.
I was happy. Not so much for myself, but for Chrissy. She'd had a lot to put up with since meeting me, and I really wanted this holiday to be something special. Very special.

We dropped the kids off at my ex-inlaws, and drove home. I had my bag to go through, again, and Chrissy had yet to pack anything. She kicked me and my case out, as apparently I was starting to do her head in. So I found myself in James' room. After spending an hour or so sorting through the contents of my bag, I knocked on the bedroom door.
"Can I come back in?"
"Are you done?"
"Think so"
"Ok, come on then"
I went in, and Chrissy was already in bed, reading some accounting book or other.
"Oh, you're in bed already?" I said.
"Duh, yeah, its like half past ten already"
"It is?" Holy fuck.
"Yeah, it is. I can't believe it took you this long to pack a bag"

Oh, I can….

"Yeah, me neither…" I said, and changed into my pj's. After I'd brushed my teeth, I checked my phone; messages from mum, Steve, and Helen. Mum and Steve just wishing me a good trip, and Helen… Apparently wasn't impressed with how today went. Fuck her, I wasn't in the mood. Ignore.

"Everything ok?"

"Yeah, just perfect" *She looks sexy as fuck in those glasses.*

"Thanks"

Talking out loud again. Cringe.

Time to check the fuck out.

I put my headphones in and went off to see Holmes and Watson.

Day 16, Monday, 25th of June.

Hmmm… I woke with a sense of trepidation. Something I always seemed to do when there was travel involved. Nerves. Fear of something going wrong. Ugh. I hated it. I looked over at Chrissy; the vision of beauty, even when sleeping. She looked calm. She looked like she hadn't a care in the world. I wish I had even 1% of her confidence.

I went downstairs and made myself a coffee. Oh, I need to call the headmaster. I retrieved the piece of paper with his number on it from the fridge and sat down to gather the strength to make the call. Why am I so weak? Why are you so weak? Jesus, it's just a fucking phone call, get on with it. Easy for you to say…

Ok. Dial number… Ringing…

"Hello?"

"Mr Jackson? It's Jack Beckett"

"Ah, morning Jack"

"Morning sir, do you have a quick minute?"

"Of course, what's on your mind? Elsie is doing ok isn't she?"

"Yes sir, she's doing just fine thank you"

"That's good to hear"

"Actually, it is about Elsie, and James. I need to take them out of school for a few hours today to see a counselor"

"A counselor?"

"Yes sir, the divorce is affecting them in ways I can't understand, so I have arranged an hour each for them with a counselor, and she's only free this morning"

"Ah, yes, of course. Never know how these things affect the young minds eh"

"No sir. I'll pick them up at nine, and have them back after lunch. Hope that is ok?"

"Of course, I'll speak to their teachers and let them know"
"Thank you sir"
"Not a problem Jack"
We dialed off. My heart was bashing away in my chest. Jesus, why were these things so difficult for me?? It was done. I took a breath, and went up for a shower.
Chrissy was up and about when I got out, and went straight in after me "Morning" she winked, walking past me naked. *Holy fu.... Shush.*
I got dressed, and made us both some toast, and a nice cup of tea. I knew she'd be busy ding her hair, so I took it upstairs for her.
"Lifesaver" she said, taking a bite of toast.
I left her to it, and went down to have my breakfast ng the garden. It was warm already, the sun hadn't hit the garden yet, but I could feel its effects already. Or maybe I was just nervous about this morning. How would the kids react? Would they be ok with it? I hoped so. I think they need someone impartial to talk to. It had helped me after all.
About ten minutes later, Chrissy came out to find me "Ah, that's where you're hiding"
"You got me"
"Nervous? It's going to be ok, you know that right? She's great at this stuff"
"I know. Still nervous though. More about hot the kids are going to react"
"They're great kids Jack, they will be fine"
"I know you're right, but still…"
"I know. Come on, we should get going"
"Ok. Let's go"
Twenty minutes later, we were sat in the car with one excited child, and one obviously worried looking child. James didn't look too happy. Shit. I fucking knew it. It's all going to go to shit. *Don't be a douche. Chill out. Just talk to him.*

The drive into PB took a while, as it was peak traffic time. It was just prolonging the agony. I needed to get out of this car and talk to my son. Come on!!!

Chrissy put her hand on my shoulder "Relax. We're almost there"

It relaxed me. A little bit. It took ages to find somewhere to park, and I thought we were going to be late. Fuck! Fuck! Fuck! I hate the city.

When we'd parked, I asked Chrissy to walk ahead with Ello so I could chat with James.

"Hey mate, you ok?"

He took a breath. "No, I'm not dad"

I put an arm around him "What's up? Is it this thing this morning?" Please say no, please say no!

"No, I'm ok with this, it'll be nice to talk to someone"

Oh, thank fuck. "What's up then? Mum?"

His head dropped. "I don't want to live with her dad, I really don't"

"Mate, I know. And you know there's nothing I can do about it right?"

"I know, but its really shit"

That hit me hard. I'd never heard my son swear before. It must be bad. But, there was nothing I could do about it.

"I know it is mate. You need to be there for your sister though"

"Why though?"

"Because that's what men do mate. It sounds terribly old fashioned, but it is what we do. We look after our women. How do you think your sister would feel if you lived at mine, and she was at your mothers?"

"Pretty bad"

"Pretty bad, yes. This is what being a man is all about, making sacrifices, being there for people"

"Being a man is shit" he laughed.

"I know it is bud, it's really fucking shit sometimes" I laughed. Dammit! I swore!
He took it in his stride, and seemed to have cheered up a bit. He ran up ahead and took Ello's hand. Chrissy dropped back and walked with me.
"Everything ok?"
"Yeah, he's fed up with living at Helen's"
"Yeah, I know. He just needs to get it off his chest every now and again. It's important that you're there for him. You do a good job Jack Beckett"
"Thank you Christelle Lenoir"
I took her hand, and we walked into the station. The kids were very excited with their visitor lanyards, and made a real pint of showing everyone they walked past as we made our way up to Katy's office. She welcomed us warmly, and sat us down.
"Hey guys, I just wanted to have a quick group chat, just to go through what I'll be doing this morning"
We sat for ten minutes or so as she did exactly that. When it was time for child one to go in, Ello volunteered.
"Ok, I'll take James on a tour of the station" Chrissy said. "You wanna come, or have a coffee?"
"I'll have a coffee if you don't mind, I need to calm my nerves."
"Ok, cool, come on then, I'll drop you at the canteen"
She left me there with a large coffee, and went off with an excited James to tour the station. Bless her, she really was good with them. I sat and did my usual; over think things.
To take my mind off things, I called Kyle to see how things were going. He was good enough to talk to me for fifteen minutes or so, and at the end of the call, I was calm again. He had everything under control, and Irene was in the office with him. Though it wouldn't be a regular occurrence.
That made me happy. He would be able to coach her through how we did things in person rather than try do it remotely. He was living up to my expectations.

I sat and watched one f the video's she had completed for review. Wow, she'd nailed it. I don't know why I was expecting her not to, but I was really impressed regardless. I text Kyle a thumbs up emoji. Another thing I didn't need to worry about anymore.

My coffee had gone cold by the time I'd finished, and Chrissy came back with James shortly after.

"Hey, enjoy that?"

"Yeah, they locked me in a cell!"

"Wow, let's hope that's the only time that happens" I winked. I gave him my card, "Go treat yourself prisoner" He smiled and went off to the counter to fill up a tray with crap no doubt.

"You good?" Chrissy asked.

"Yeah, I'm ok. I spoke to Kyle, and it seems Irene is doing really well. She even came into the office this morning"

"Wow, that must have been difficult for her"

"Yeah, probably easier because I wasn't there"

"probably. You're better then?"

"Yeah, I am. Thanks for being so good today"

"Hey, I'm good every day"" she winked.

"Yes. Yes you are"

Katy walked in with Ello just as James sat down with his tray of goodies. "Oh man"

Katy smiled "You can bring it with you. Come on"

That made him happy, and they left together, tray and all.

"Hey, you ok?" I asked Ello.

"Yes thank you daddy" she said, looking over to the food counter.

"Come on, let's get you a tray of badness too" Chrissy said, and took her over.

I smiled contentedly as the two women in my life walked hand in hand across to the food counter. She's such a good kid. *And Chrissy?* What a woman. *Amen brother, amen.*

My heart swelled with love watching the two of them together.

I was thankful that they got on so well. It could have been VERY different.
They cam back over, and we sat talking about this and that whilst Ello shovelled crap down her throat. Thank god it was a rare occurrence! I'd be taking her back to school on a massive sugar high. Sorry teachers! Chrissy suggested a tour to Ello, and she gladly accepted. This time, I tagged along. There's only so much coffee a man can take…
The tour was good; it was amazing to see how well liked Chrissy was by all the staff at the cop shop. It shouldn't really surprise me, but it did nevertheless. She found another willing volunteer to take us around, and what a tour it was! Ello loved locking me up in a cell, and pretending to have lost the key. Lol. They let me out eventually, but only after I promised to be really good from now on.
We finished our tour outside Katy's office, and waited for James to come out. When he did, some five minutes later, Katy motioned for me to join her. I followed her into the office.
"Sit, jack, I don't bite"
Sorry, just nervous"
"Relax. Your kids are incredibly resilient. You know what their biggest worry is?"
"No?" I was worried now. What the fuck could it be? Helen probably.
"You"
It hit me like a bomb. Me? What?
"Me?"
"Yes. They're incredibly worried about you Jack. I gather your health hasn't been to good lately?"
I told her about the fainting, and mental health problems.
"I'm glad to hear you're speaking to someone about it, and that your health is on th up" she smiled. "So many men don't, and that only leads to bad things"
"Yes, I know" I said.

"Don't worry about them Jack; they're gong to be fine. Concentrate on getting yourself back on top; it's what they want most"

Relief hit me like a tsunami. They were worried about me. Of course, that worried me, but I was relived they weren't worried about the divorce, Helen, the living arrangements, school. Wow.

"They're good kids. You're a lucky man Jack"

"Thank you"

"And Chrissy seems very happy"

"Yeah, she is I think. She's very good with them"

"Yeah, I can see that." she smiled. "Thank you"

"For what?"

"For making her better. I've never seen her so happy"

I blushed "Erm, thanks"

"I mean it. Look at her, she's radiant. You've done well"

"I hope it's only going to get better" I said.

"I'm sure it will" she held out a hand, and I shook it. "Take care of your family by taking care of yourself"

"Thank you, I will"

We left as a happy family. Chrissy had even managed to score a Police cap for each of the kids.

Ok. It's done. And, as usual, it wasn't nearly as bad as I had imagined.

After saying goodbye to the kids, and promising to bring back presents from Italy, we left them at school and drove home. I closed the door and threw myself onto the sofa. Wow. What a day already, and it was only lunchtime. Bag. Gotta check bag. I dragged myself off the sofa and went upstairs.

I'd gone through my bag several times already of course, making sure I had bare essentials; I didn't want to make my usual mistake of over-packing massively. Most importantly, I triple checked I had the ring in my carry-on bag. It was there. All three times I checked. *Fucking told you, didn't I?*

"Hey, you happy?" Chrissy said, indicating my bag "You've packed about six times now"
"Yeah, think so. I usually take far too much so I wanted to make sure I did it right this time. You packed?"
"Yep, did it yesterday morning when you were out. I'm ready to go"
"Wow, organised"
"Not really, we fly this evening dumbass"
"Hmmm. You think I need…" she cut me off.
"Stop. Leave your bag, its fine. I'm sure you have whatever you'll need."
"Yeah, ok. You're right" I zipped it up and she took it away.
"I'll go put them in the boot so you can't touch it"
Lol, she owns you.
Fuck you. I checked my watch; 4 hours till we leave for the airport. We were going to park at the airport, rather than faffing with a train, I wanted minimal stress.
She came back in, kissed me, and said "Don't stress. It's going to be amazing"
"I know, sorry"
"Don't be, just relax."
I took a breath. "I'll be ok"
"I know you will, I'll make sure of it" *Oh yeah? Wink wink, nudge nudge.* Shut up you dick.
"I'll try my best"
"Hey, come with me" she said.
"What?"
"Come on" she took my hand and dragged me into the living room. "Someone once taught me something I want to try with you" she went over to the hifi, and pushed a few buttons.
"Ready?"
She pressed play, and Feeder came blasting out of the speakers.
"Just let go" she shouted, and started jumping around like an idiot. I laughed, and joined in.

Getting a taste of my own medicine felt weird, but I felt far better afterwards; the stress had disappeared.
"Better?" she asked, panting
"Better" I said, and kissed her. "Thanks"
"Works for me every time" she winked.
"Factual" I agreed.
She was right of course; I felt miles better, and she knew it.
"Right" she said. "Ready?"
"Ready"
We double checked the house, I called Steve to make sure he didn't forget to feed tha cat, and we jumped in the car.
"Drive" Chrissy said, putting on her sunglasses.
It had been a while since I'd driven, and I was looking forward to it.

The drive to the airport was uneventful, and the eternity we sat around waiting at the airport was made easier with a beer or two at the bar. The flight itself only took just over two hours. Not that I'd noticed; I'd fallen asleep as soon as we were in the air.
It was dark by the time we landed, so I don't get to see any of the surrounding area from the sky. It was however, still very warm when we walked out of the terminal building. We caught a taxi to the hotel, and checked in. *Holy fuck. What a hotel!* Jesus. Posh is an understatement. It was opulence itself. And our suite! Holy fuck. It was massive, and fantastic. We had a balcony overlooking the river too!
"I don't even want to ask how much this cost" I said to Chrissy, holding her in my arms on the balcony.
"Please don't" she laughed "You'd have a heart attack."
The view from the balcony was beautiful, as was the woman in my arms. Things couldn't be more perfect.

Laying in bed, I didn't have any badness to dwell on, and I hadn't even packed my headphones. I didn't need them. Everything I needed was right here. Well, almost everything. Kids were hundreds of miles away, living somewhere they didn't want to be. That was a problem for another day though.

Now I wanted to sleep. Needed to sleep. I couldn't wait to get up in the morning and explore this place. I was in Italy! Yes! I had checked I still had the ring earlier. Now I just needed to find the right time to ask this gorgeous woman to marry me. And then hope she'd say yes.
Of course she will.
You reckon?
Trust me mate, she will.
Ok, we'll see.
Dude, relax. You're getting all worried again. Chill.
Yeah, you're right.

Sleep.

Day 17, Tuesday, 26th of June.

We were awake pretty early. The sun was shining through the open windows, and the soft white curtains were blowing gently in the morning breeze. Next to me, Chrissy was still asleep. She had apparently taken her top off during the night, and just had a pair of linen pj shorts on. It had been hot during the night; I was only wearing my boxers, so couldn't blame her. I got up, got myself a bottle of cold water from the fridge, and sat out on the balcony. It was beautiful. I had seen the view yesterday evening, if it looked beautiful then, it looked stunning now, in the early morning light. We were in an extremely nice hotel called the Lungarno, situated on the river between two bridges (Ponte Santa Trinita and the Ponte Vecchio). Our room was on the river, so the view was to die for. People were milling about, and the odd scooter buzzed by. We were far enough away for it not to disturb us; which was a blessing. Florence. Wow. Never thought I'd ever be sat here. Not somewhere I'd thought about; this was Chrissy's choice. We'd only been here since yesterday evening, but I loved it already. I took a deep breath, filling my lungs with the sweet morning.
"Morning" she had appeared behind me and put her arms around me. Resting her head on my shoulder she said "It's beautiful isn't it?"
"Yeah, it sure is" *Wait a minute, can I feel what I think I can feel?* Yes. *Oh my…*
My perverted inner voice was referring to the feeling of her bare chest on my back; she was still topless. I loved the fact that she didn't care.
"Let's have breakfast here" she said.
"Good idea. I'm in no rush to leave"

She went off to call reception and arrange it. "You want OJ and coffee?"

"Yes please"

When she re-appeared, she had a top on. Probably only because we'd ordered room service.

She sat next to me, and put her legs up resting on mine.

"I'm liking this hotel" I said "the view is amazing"

"Yeah, it's quite something" Pause. She sighed. "You are talking about the actual view right?"

"Sure, that too"

A knock at the door saved me from a shoulder punch. "You're lucky" she said, getting up.

She opened the door, and greeted the waiter in perfect sounding Italian. Well, I'm no expert, but it sounded flawless to me. The waiter certainly reacted as such. He took great pride in preparing our table with breakfast, while Chrissy quizzed him about places to go and eat (so she told me after). I couldn't really follow, but they seemed to be getting on very well. When he was finished, he asked if there was anything else he could do. Chrissy said he'd done more than enough, and we were extremely grateful. She tipped him extremely generously, and he left extremely happy. "Ciao Bella"

"Everything ok?" I asked

"Yep, got lots of good tips on where to go, and restaurants the locals consider good."

"That's always useful" I agreed. "He seemed happy"

"It pays to be friendly with the staff. No, ugh, I hate that word. The local people? You never know what they can do for you"

I laughed "I know exactly what you mean. Let's eat"

The table looked fantastic, set out with bread, meats, pastries, boiled eggs, orange juice, and coffee.

We took our time, in true Italian fashion, chatting about how we were going to fill our day, and (more importantly) where we would eat.

The weather was glorious, and humdrum of local routing was gently filtering in and out from across the river. What an absolutely beautiful place.

"Yes it is" Chrissy agreed. I wasn't aware I'd said that out loud, but I do have a habit of doing that.

"I'm going to jump in the shower" I said, looking for a quick escape.

"I'm going to sit here and finish my coffee" she said, leaning back in her chair, the sun on her face. She looked so beautiful. I had a quick shower, and got dressed. Chrissy had jumped in the shower after me, so I took a bit of time to check in with Kyle. We had a lot of work this week, and I wanted to make sure he was doing ok with it. All was going well, he was on-track to finish Friday. I said I could help out Friday, as I'd be home Thursday afternoon. All good there. I thought about when the right moment would be to propose, but couldn't make my mind up. I carried the small box with me all day, just in case.

Chrissy was ready to go; hair tied back in a simple pony tail, white linen top, floral skirt, sandals. Beauty. Me; khaki shorts, white t, flip-flops. Standard summer rig.

We set off into the old centre of Florence, which was actually easy to navigate as it was set out in a sort of grid pattern. Naturally, we made for the cathedral of St Maria. We were in-line behind a contingent of American tourists, and there were a few other groups milling around. We walked inside, and were immediately struck by its beauty. I'm not a religious person in the slightest, but I can appreciate beauty. The painted dome was just stunning. We stood for a while gazing up at its splendour.

"Wow"

"It's stunning isn't it?" Chrissy said.

"Yeah, and then some"

We were lucky enough to only find a short queue waiting at the entrance to the tower.

We spent the time looking around, and discussing various bits and pieces. When we finally made it up to the top, we were treated to a gorgeous view of old Florence. Awe inspiring. Almost two hours later, we walked back out into the sun.
"Fancy a coffee?" Chrissy asked "I know just the place"
We walked the short distance to the Piazza Del Republica, which has café's either end, and a lovely old merry-go-round in the middle. "In here" she said.
We took a table outside the Caffe Gilli. "I've read about this place" I said "It's supposed to be the best"
"Yep, reportedly the best coffee around"
A charming waiter came over, and Chrissy conversed with him in her fancy Italian. She asked what I wanted "What does the waiter recommend?" I asked.
He obliged, after translation, and recommended a coffee and Cuore di Amalfi, a lemon based treat. I signaled my approval, and Chrissy doubled up. The waiter bowed, and walked off into the café.
"I feel a bit like a tourist" I said "You seem to be getting on splendidly with your Italian"
"Certainly helps" she said.
"It's quite a sexy language" I remarked.
"Ooh, sir likes me speaking Italian?"
"Sir does indeed"
We laughed, and she promised to help me learn the language.
"Do you speak any languages other than English?" she asked.
"Well, I can speak Dutch, German, and some French" I said.
"Not much use here though"
"Wow, that's impressive. I only speak Italian I'm afraid"
"Where did you learn?" I asked. She looked uneasy.
"I have a confession"
"Go on"
"I went to university here"
"Here? In Florence?"

"Yep. I did an accounting degree, two years"
"No wonder you know your way around" I said. Kind of explained things a bit. "That must have been amazing"
"Yes, it was wonderful"
"I thought you said you'd always wanted to go to Florence?" I said. She had used those words.
"A white lie. I wanted to bring you here because it's so beautiful"
"I'm not complaining" I said, sipping my coffee (Which was fucking AWESOME by the way)
I ate a bit of the lovely looking lemon pastry "Mmmm. Oh my god, this is good" I said. It was like an explosion of summer in my mouth. "But I guess you knew that already" I winked.
"Yeah, a personal favourite"
"Any more surprises?" I asked.
"Like?" she responded, puzzled.
"Dunno, I guess I don't know a lot about you"
"Same here. Let's spend some time talking"
"Fine by me" I said, looking around the idyllic setting.
"Tell me about your education" she asked
"Well, I went to school in Ramsey, then did A-levels in Peterborough"
"What subjects?" she asked, taking the opportunity to eat.
"Mm" I said, finishing my coffee "English, Maths, Physics, Business Studies, History"
"You did 5 A levels?" she asked, clearly shocked.
"What can I say, I'm clever"
"Wow. I'm impressed. Uni?"
"I did my honours degree in Plymouth, three years"
"Plymouth?"
"Yep, seemed like a good choice, and it was"
"What did you study?"
"Electronic Communications Engineering"
"Sounds fancy, and difficult"

"It wasn't easy for sure, but I made it through" I said.
"Sounds cool" she smiled.
"How about you?"
"School and college in Peterborough, *only* 3 A-levels; English, Business Studies and Maths. Then Uni here for two years, accounting degree, followed by a Masters in Portsmouth Uni"
"Masters? Wow, now *that* is impressive"
"Thank you, needed for the job to be honest, it's quite specialised"
"I can imagine. How come Florence?"
"Me and a friend decided to go there together after we finished our A levels, she's from here, and was very persuasive" she ended with a giggle.
"Must have been difficult, language wise"
"Yes, it was. She had been teaching me a bit of Italian over the years, and the Uni were very good. They always asked if I had understood what had been covered, and I did extra Italian classes in the evening"
"Wow. That is good"
"Yeah" she said "Well, that was good, we know a bit more about each other"
"Yep, it is" I said "Good to know I'm in such illustrious company"
"Says the guy with five A levels"
It was a good chat, and kind of reminded me of how little we knew about each other. Seemed wrong, but we'd never really sat down and talked about ourselves. I wasn't interested in past relationships or stuff like that; just who she was. I didn't know that much about her. And she knew very little about me in turn.
"Hey" I said "Would you mind if we did a bit of a question and answer session over dinner tonight?"
"Not at all, about what?"
"Ourselves. I'm curious about you, and want to know more about you" I said.

"Same here. Sounds like fun" she smiled.

We settled up, and wandered around the rustic streets of the old city.

"Your friend still live here?" I asked.

"Sadly no, she lives in New York now, big shot job"

"Wow, good for her. And here you are in Ramsey Forty Foot" I laughed.

"I'm perfectly happy" she said, squeezing my hand. Now? *No, not the right moment.* Sure? *Trust me, wait.* The ring was weighing heavy in my pocket, and I was paranoid about losing it.

We wandered in and out of some lovely boutique shops, and Chrissy bought a few bits and pieces. It was a lovely afternoon, she took me to see her old university, where we had a drink in the cafeteria. It brought back a lot of memories for her, which was nice to see.

We then caught a taxi to the Basilica of San Miniato al Monte, which was absolutely beautiful. The panels lining the walls inside were stunning, incredibly vibrant. The views were also amazing; it was located on the top of a hill, with incredible views of the city and surrounding area.

"Good thing we got a taxi" I said "Wouldn't fancy walking up here in this weather"

"Yeah, wouldn't have been pleasant" Chrissy agreed. We found a place in the shade and sat for a while, just enjoying the view. I took a bottle of water from my backpack, and handed it to her.

"Oh, thanks, I'm thirsty as hell" she said gratefully, and took a long swig of water. Now? This is a good place? Yes, perfect. Ok, cool! I put my hand in my pocket and pulled out the box whilst she was admiring the views. I got ready, opened it, and… Fuck. *What?* The ring. It's not in the box. *Of course not, you took it out earlier and put it in the zipped pocket in the bag.* Which is in the hotel room, fuck. *You absolute fucking idiot.*

"Wow, it's truly stunning here." she commented "But also hot" she laughed. You ready to go?"

Flustered, I said "Yeah, sure, where to next?"
"Don't know about you, but I'm kind of done for the day. I was thinking maybe go back to the hotel and get a late lunch somewhere?" Fuck aye, that works for me.
"Blinder. I'm up for that" It was almost half past one, and I was quite hungry. "Any ideas?"
"I do know a few places, but we're talking almost 15 years ago"
"Why don't we just have a wander and find somewhere"
"Sounds like a plan, I'll get us an uber" she arranged the taxi on her phone "5 minutes"
The taxi dropped us back at the hotel, and we went up to our room to drop bags off and to freshen up. *Get the ring.* Not feeling it, I'll do it when we get back later. I'll take her for a drink in the bar and do it there. *Good plan.* Half hour later, we were out front, looking for somewhere to eat. We turned right, and started walking, and found a place called Cammillo just down the street.
It was quite busy, but there were a few empty tables. Chrissy worked her magic, flashed a few smiles, and got us a table. We were very lucky to get in apparently.
"Well done Lenoir" I said.
"Welcome" she smiled.
I picked up the menu, and instantly realised I needed more help; it was all in Italian. The waiter came over with some water, and Chrissy worked her usual charm.
"He recommended the Malfatti"
"The what?"
"They're basically ricotta and spinach dumplings"
"Hmm, sounds a bit heavy for lunch" I said
"He also recommended an English menu" she said "He's bringing one over"
"Who's the dick now?"
"Yeah, me. Sorry. I also ordered Rose if that's ok?"
"Rose suits me fine" I said.

The waiter dutifully appeared a minute or so later with two glasses of wine and a menu for me.

"Better?" she laughed.

"Better. Thanks"

I looked through the menu, but was struggling to find something light for lunch.

"You ok?"

"Yeah, I just want something light, and it all looks pretty heavy going"

"I'll find out" she stuck her hand up, and the waiter appeared. They had an animated discussion about it, lots of hand gestures. After he left, with a huge smile on his face, she told me he was going to put together a selection of taster dishes.

"That sounds good to me" I said.

"Yeah, we get to try quite a few dishes, so all the better"

"Cheers to that" I said, raising my glass.

"Cheers" she raised hers to mine.

Needless to say, lunch was delicious. We had a platter with ten different small portions. It was exquisite. Not too filling, just right. The ring was weighing heavy enough on my mind…

We got back to our room, and crashed on the bed. "Pffff, I'm knackered" she said, yawning

"Yeah, me too" I agreed.

"Siesta?" she suggested.

"Good idea"

I set a timer for an hour, and we had a well-deserved nap. I slept badly though, nerves were getting the best of me. When would be the best time?

Would she actually say yes?

What? Oh my god.

What are you thinking? Shut up. Of course she'll say yes.

Of course she will.

Won't she?

What?

Kidding, rack out time.
Knob.
When the alarm went off, Chrissy was first out of bed. I stretched for a bit, and joined her out on the balcony. The sun was getting lower in the sky, but it was still quite warm.
"I got you some water" she said, gesturing at a cold bottle on the table.
"Cheers, could have slept right through" I said, yawning. I picked up the bottle and drank greedily.
"Oh stop, you have me yawning now she said"
"What time were you thinking for dinner?" I asked.
"I booked a table for eight, hope that's ok?" she said.
"You did? When?" I asked.
"This morning, that nice gentleman gave me a top recommendation"
"Wow, ok."
"Not good?" she asked, worried.
"No, no, all good. You are quite amazing, you know that?"
"Yeah, I know" she winked.
"I love you" I said, and kissed her. "Drink in the bar before dinner?"
"I love you too, drink sounds amazing" she smiled. "Right, I'm off for a shower"
"Ok, I'll just check in with the kids"
"Excellent idea" she said, and went off to the bathroom.
I text the kids, and chatted with them whilst she was in the shower. It felt good to know the kids were ok. I went to my bag, and put the ring in the pocket of the chinos I was going to wear. There. I know where it is. In the bar. *Deep breath Jack.* I know. I'm nervous though. *No need matey, no need.*
I sat out on the balcony, and reflected on the day. All in all, we'd had a nice day out; sight-seeing, bit of shopping, nice lunch; it was superb. Tonight was the night, I didn't want to put it off any longer. My stomach was somersaults.

Chrissy had just finished in the shower, so I reluctantly left my cosy seat and had a shower myself.

A nice cool shower was just what I needed; it took my mind off the proposal, which was just messing with my head. The butterflies in my stomach were going like the clappers. Dammit. Stop. I was busy drying off when Chrissy called me from the bedroom.

"Jack, could you help me with something for a sec please?" I wrapped myself in the towel, and went to see what she wanted. I opened the door, and…

"Holy fucking shit"

"Could you help me out of this please, amore mio?" she said demurely.

She was dressed in the most beautiful lingerie I'd ever seen. Stockings, suspenders, the lot.

Jesus fucking Christ.

She looked amazing.

Fucking understatement. You're about to get VERY lucky.

Yeah, time for you to disappear; this is all me.

I dropped the towel and stepped forward "With pleasure Madame…"

The End.

Outro.

Oh my God. It's done. Four parts. Wow. What did you think of this part? They finally got it on, hooray! Hooray!
I really hope you enjoyed this, and the preceding three books. Basically the story as a whole. I'd like to think it's not the worst thing ever committed to paper, but have no illusions that it is the work of genius either. I like it, and I enjoyed writing it. I had considered another part, Jack still has to pop the question after all, but decided against it. I've got all the shit out of my head. There's nothing left.
As I progressed from part one to four, it got harder and harder to remember small details like names, appointments, things that had been said, etc. There was a lot of going back through the preceding books to ensure I got stuff right, and remembered to do things that I said I would earlier in the story. Make sense? It was frustrating.
Example?
The Cello! Ugh. When Fleur arrived on the scene, they were talking in the garden, singing Spice Girls songs? Fleur was surprised at Chrissy doing running. I had to flick back through to see if I'd said anything about Chrissy exercising in book 1. When I did, I saw the thing about her playing the Cello, and realised I hadn't used it at all since they'd met. Hence I just made her say she'd sold it. Easy way out.
Hence; I'm done with the 17 Days series, milked it or all its worth. Soz.
As a consolation…...
Want a taster of the new series I'm writing? It's called Loyalty and Honour. The first chapter can be found at the end of this book. Have a read, I'm really excited about it. It gets better and better as the book goes on, trust me.

Acknowledgements.

My proof reader Sarah. Thank You doesn't ever seem to quite cover it. As I mentioned, I don't read these books after writing them, so I don't see grammar/wrong words, etc. I do a quick spell-check, nothing else. The only reason people are able to read a coherent, grammatically correct book is because of you and your infamous red pen. *Red pen wanker!*
And… You came up with the name for Jack's bar! Kudos. Gratitude.

My Writing Journey.

Allow me a minor tangent about my writing journey…for the 17 Days Series.
Just humour me.
When I first started writing in 2023, I never thought I'd get to the point where I had 6 completed books a year later. Yes, apart from the 4 in this series, I have written another 2.
People keep telling me it's amazing and how much they admire such creativity. Personally, I don't think it's that hard. Anyone could do it. Think of a character, and a loose story idea, then pad it out. My first effort was a Sherlock Holmes story. Characters already existed, to a certain extent. I made up additional key characters myself. It's not the best adventure the great detective has ever had, and I apologise for that to him and his devoted fans, but it's mine. I wrote it. It came from my mind. My creation. There's something stupidly pride inspiring about that. When I first started writing 17 Days, I had an idea of a guy, coming out of a shitty divorce, and basically on a journey to recover his shattered mind. I wanted to show that men ARE affected by divorce. It doesn't get publicity, because, let's face it; everyone loves a crying female victim right.

Borderline sexism! Sorry. No offence at all, believe me. It just frustrates me that women are always seen as the victims in divorce. Automatically. Regardless of what people know about what really happened. Grrrr. Also, men are automatically thought of as being cold hearted automatons without feelings. We are not. We may not always show emotions, but they're in there. Oh, they are in there alright.
Regardless of being male or female, divorce causes hurt. It causes pain.

It can drive people towards a regrettable solution. If you haven't been through it, it's difficult to understand.

Anyway, back to the creative process. Yeah, so, I never thought that story would turn into a series of four books. When my wife Angela first read a draft, she gave me encouraging feedback. Most notably; the relationship between Jack and Steve. This gave me what I needed; if there was something good about it, then I should write more. And so I did. There was more feedback from my proof reader Sarah, which was more of an emotional response (hope that's ok to say?). The story had an emotional effect. Yes! Exactly what I'd hoped for. Most of the stuff in these books is REAL, and *deserves* an emotional response.

A couple of general impressions/misconceptions:

This story is about your life.

Nope. Well, ok, some of it is, not going to lie. Maybe more than "some"… There is a lot of shit buried deep inside me, and a lot of it is reflected in these pages. However, I know quite a few divorcees, and we talk. Their experiences are in here too. It's an amalgamation of men's experiences with divorce and subsequent depression. The Social Anxiety is mine, I have no reservations about admitting to that. I suck in social situations, and they fill me with complete and utter dread. As for the rest; I know which bits are about me, but that's for me alone to know. Despite being able to write this long story, depicting outgoing/extroverted personalities, I'm actually a quiet, private person. No shock there to people that actually know me I'm sure.

You must make a load of money from these books.

LOL! No. Each one of these books will cost more to publish that I will make back. Why? The cover. It's not my picture; I have to pay to use it. Each of the 4 covers had to be paid for separately. But, that doesn't bother me at all.

It's a great photograph, which encapsulates what the book is about; a broken man on the floor with a woman walking away, not giving a shit. Thank you to the photographer, I love it and don't mind paying to use it.

It's not about the money anyway. It's about other people, be they people I know, or strangers, reading something I created. Every time I finish a book, or check my sales/read stats, I feel an immense sense of pride. I'm proud of myself. I created something. As I write this, only the first 2 parts are for sale. How many copies sold? Not many. But that doesn't matter. Copies have been sold. That's what matters. And I've received good feedback. It's difficult to put into words how that feels.

How's about a few readers questions?

How do you come up with the story line?
Easily. Nah, kidding. Sort of.

The characters turned out great, and their parts/stories easily established based on experiences. To answer the question though; at the time of writing this Outro, I've actually only written 11 pages of this book. I wrote the final Chapter first, then started at Day 1. I wrote 2 days, then wrote the first part of Day 16. Then I went back to Day 3. I finished the breakfast part of Day 4, then changed the end based on the events of Day 3. Confuzzled? Me too.

Why write the end first? I already knew exactly what the last 5 or so sentences were going to be, so I wrote those down and created the rest of the chapter leading up to them.

For book one, the ending came to me only a few days into the book. Same for the second one. Book 3 is different; there is no cliff-hanger ending like the other two. There was a reason for this obviously; the time difference between book 3 and 4 was about a month or so.

Can't really write a cliff-hanger for such a timespan.

Hence, it just ends. I did write the parent evening ending about half way or so through the book. It just came to me, and seemed a good place to stop. It then just wrote the rest leading up to it. Something to aim for I guess. Kind of helps as you can use if in the story leading up to the event.

Have you read your own books?
Nope. I've been asked that by a few people. I can't bring myself to do it in-case I don't like them. My excuse is; I wrote them, why would I need to read them? I will though. One day. Also, too many memories. Uncomfortable.

Thanks for reading, and take care of yourselves.
Mike.

Carry on reading for the first chapter of my new book Loyalty and Honour...

Loyalty and Honour; Chapter 1. The Hospital.

Sound was the first sense to come back. He could hear shuffling, coughing, and birdsong. Next came smell, it smelled medicinal, clinical. Where was he? He focused on opening his eyes. It was a struggle. A small amount of light filtered in; bright. Very bright. Shapes moved around, out of focus. Damn. Why was it so bright? Slowly but surely, his vision returned to normal. Behind him was a large open window, which explained the birdsong. He looked around, and saw he was in a large, narrow hall, lined on two sides with beds. All the beds were occupied by men. Wounded men. Was he in hospital? Where? And, perhaps more importantly… Why?
A shape stopped at the foot of his bed; a nurse.
"Ah, nice to see you finally awake Rottenführer Deckman"
Deckman? Yes. That was my name! Joseph Deckman, Corporal in the Waffen SS.
I cleared my throat "Where am I?"
"You are in the Hohenlychen Sanatorium" she said.
Where? Wait. I had heard of it. An SS Hospital, near… Near… Shit. Where was it? Berlin! Of course. But why was I here? I felt a dull pain in my leg, and I tried to sit up to see what it was. Tried, but failed. A searing pain in my leg prevented me sitting up fully and I fell back in frustration.
"Your leg" the nurse said, sensing my anxiety "Don't worry, it's still there"
I let out a loud sigh of relief.
"They all do that you know" she said "Check for amputations"
"It's still there" I said.

"Yes, it is" she said "You're lucky, a bit higher and you wouldn't be here"
"What?" I couldn't remember what had happened.
"The bullet. It missed the artery and lodged in the thigh bone"
"I was shot?" I was shot??? What? Where? When? How?
"I presume so, hence the bullet" she smiled "You'll be fine tough. Your memory will return in time. A week or so, and you'll be out of here"
"How long have I been here?"
"Three days, not long" she signed the sheet on the clipboard and went to walk away, but stopped. "Oh, I forget. You have a visitor, he's been waiting to see you for two days"
"A visitor?" A visitor? Here? Who? Couldn't be my parents, they were in… In… Dammit. Austria! Yes, they lived in Austria.
"Yes, a Hauptsturmführer Wiezinge"
A Captain? Waiting for me? A mere Corporal? What was going on? I couldn't recall ever meeting a Captain Wiezinge.
"I don't know who that is" I said.
"Well, he seems to know who you are. Maybe seeing him will help with your memory?"
"Perhaps"
"If you are up to seeing him, I can fetch him for you now?" she asked.
I nodded, and arranged my bed and pyjamas as she walked out of the ward.

I heard him long before I saw him, his boots sounding loudly on the stone floor, echoing around the tiled ward. The sound grew louder and louder until he turned the corner and walked into the ward. His crisp uniform gave an aura of importance and style. How smart it looked.
I remembered suddenly why I had wanted to join the SS; the uniform. I had visited Berlin with my parents in 1936, and had seen one of the many parades.

There were hundreds of black clad soldiers of the Leibstandarte SS Adolf Hitler marching in unison, their hobnailed boots stomping loudly on the cobbled street. What a sight it had been! I knew right then that I wanted to be one of them. Against the wishes of my parents, I had joined the SS Standarte Der Führer as soon as I could. It had been hard work, and the selection process intense, but I had been accepted. There were questions about my mother, of course, but she had taken German citizenship after her marriage to my father. Still, the doubt was obvious in their faces. Regardless, I had gotten in! I had been part of the invasion of Poland, and then… And then? Grrr! I couldn't remember.

How had I ended up here? If only my memory would work! The loud footsteps ended abruptly as the Captain found my bed. He snapped his heels together sharply and his right arm shot up in salute. "Heil Hitler!"

I stiffened up, and returned his salute as best I could "Hauptsturmführer" I did not recognise the man.

"At ease Rottenführer" he said. He removed his peaked cap, placed his black gloves inside it, and set it down on the bed. He opened a briefcase, and removed several objects; some letters, two envelopes, and a case. Medals. For me? Why?

He picked up a piece of paper, cleared his throat, and read loudly: "Rottenführer Deckman, it is with honour and pride that I present on behalf of the Führer Adolf Hitler, and the grateful German people, the Verwundetenabzeichen Schwartz for being wounded in combat" he took the badge from is package, and placed it on the bed next to me. Wound badge. I should have expected it; it was presented to all wounded soldiers. You had to have been wounded twice; this was my second time. I had been wounded during the invasion of Poland a few years earlier. Yes! I remember now! Shrapnel wound to the right shoulder.

He picked up another piece of paper, and repeated the ritual; "Rottenführer Deckman, it is with honour and pride that I present on behalf of the Führer Adolf Hitler, and the grateful German people, the Allgemeine Sturmabzeichen Silber for showing exceptional bravery in combat" Again, he placed the badge on the bed next to me.

He picked up another piece of paper, smiled, and read again "Rottenführer Deckman, it is with honour and pride that I present on behalf of the Führer Adolf Hitler, and the grateful German people, the Ritterkreuz". He beamed with pride as he pinned the heavy Knights Cross to my pyjama top. He promptly snapped off another salute, accompanied by applause from those capable of doing so in the ward.

He shook my hand "Congratulations Deckman. It is a great honour to receive the Knights Cross"

"Thank you Sir" The Knights Cross???

"Would you permit me to read out your commanding officers commendation?" he asked.

"Not at all" Please do, I thought. I can't remember a thing.

He unfolded yet another piece of paper, cleared his throat, and spoke loudly once more:

"From: Obersturmführer Rotmann II/SSDF to: SS Command; Commendation for Rottenführer Deckman.

Rottenführer Deckman was part of the raiding party led by Hauptsturmführer Kuttel that crossed the Ijssel River on May 10th 1940, to capture Fort Westervoort. Under intense enemy machine-gun fire, they crossed the river, when sadly, Hauptsturmfürer Kuttel was killed. Still under intense enemy fire, Rottenführer Deckman rallied and led the remaining men to the opposite bank, where they successfully neutralised the enemy positions, allowing the remainder of the Division to cross in safety.

Rottenführer Deckman personally took out 3 of 5 enemy machine gun positions using grenades, despite being wounded during the crossing. His conduct under fire is an example to us all. Heil Hitler. Signed: Rotmann."

There was silence in the ward, which was broken moments later by another round of applause from the other injured men, and from the captain.

"You are a shining example of an SS man" Wiezinge said whilst applauding.

"Thank you Sir" I didn't really know what to say to that. Flashes of memories returning; the whizzing of bullets, the acrid smell of cordite, the screams of dying men, the coldness of the water. Kuttel was dead. He had been my commanding officer for over a year, and I liked him a lot. His loss saddened me.

"One final piece of paper" Wiezinge said smiling "If you permit"

"Of course Hauptsturmführer"

"It is my honour to inform you of your promotion to Oberscharführer, by order of the Reichsführer himself, effective immediately" He handed me the promotion letter, and a small package containing the requisite collar and shoulder insignia. The letter was signed by Himmler himself.

"You honour me, Hauptsturmführer" I said.

"You honour us all Deckman" he smiled, and shook my hand "Congratulations"

"Thank you Sir"

He placed the commendation letters on my bedside table, and sat.

"You know, you will get a choice of posting, it comes with the Ritterkreuz"

"I do?"

"Indeed. Think carefully Deckman. This could be your ticket out of the front lines."

"But, I couldn't leave my comrades Sir" I couldn't remember my brothers in the division, but I'm sure I had some. And I sure as hell didn't want to abandon them.

He leaned towards me, looked around, and then whispered "Consider your choices Deckman. You want to carry on being cannon fodder? Our casualties are severe, especially in the lower ranks. This is your chance to get out of the firing line"

"Thank you Sir, I will think about it"

"Good man" he said, standing. He picked up his cap, and put his gloves back on. "I wish you all the best Deckman" he saluted, and turned to leave the ward. He stopped and thought for a moment, then turned to me "By the way, if you are considering taking the officer route, let me know, I will recommend you to the Jünckerschule in Bad Tolz. I'll give you my number, call if you are interested" He scribbled a number on a slip of paper and handed it to me. "Get well soon soldier" he said, smiled, and then left.

As I sat there thinking about what had just happened, I could hear his loud footsteps in the hall diminishing slowly.

The Knights Cross? Obersharführer? Officer school? Wow. What had just happened? Was it a dream? A hallucination?

Moments later, the nurse returned with a tray. "Congratulations Sergeant Deckman, I brought you some coffee and a piece of strudel to celebrate"

"That's very kind of you" I said, gathering the sheets of paper and folding them up. "News spreads fast"

"Difficult not to overhear" she smiled "His voice echoed all around the hospital. I'm pretty sure he wanted everyone to hear"

"I guess he did."

"How are you feeling?"

I considered this for a moment.

I was feeling ok, like a bit of a fraud in fact.

I should be back with my unit, fighting alongside my comrades. But I just said "I'm feeling better, can I get out of bed yet? I'm dying to go for a walk"
"No, you must rest your leg" she said sternly, shaking her head. Reluctantly, I agreed to do so, but was determined to get out of this bed as soon as I could.
"I have other patients to see, congratulations again Sergeant"
"Thank you"
And with that, she was gone. The ward fell silent once more. There was the occasional moan from one of the beds opposite, but silent otherwise.
I wondered where my comrades were right now. Still in Holland? Had we been successful? I scolded myself for not asking the Hauptsturmführer. Idiot. I felt guilty for laying here whilst they were out there fighting for our Fatherland. I picked up my new shoulder patches with the two pips. How on earth had I deserved this? When I returned to my unit I would be a squad leader, with a whole new set of responsibilities. I had some idea of what the job entailed, having been in the same unit as Obersharführer Kahn for almost two years now, and had assisted him with the running of our squad. Would I actually go back to the same unit? I had no idea. I had not received any orders that I was aware of. There was no sign of my uniform, and my bedside cabinet was empty.
I lay back and thought about the raid. It had been intense, and I was extremely lucky I hadn't been killed. A few of the boats had been sunk by gunfire, and I had dragged all of the men to the shore, with bullets whizzing around my head.
Did I want to go back to the front line? Part of me said no, you've done enough. Wounded twice. Three years of constant combat. I had only been home once in that time, and much to my parent's dismay, I had spent most of it asleep. Sleep. God, sleep was a luxury on the lines.

I has slept in wet trenches, in abandoned buildings, in a chicken coup, anywhere I could. I was permanently tired, but I suppose you don't really feel it much when your life is under constant threat.

A doctor broke me from my daydream.

"Ah, Obersharführer, how are you feeling?"

"Better, feeling good enough to get up and try my leg" I said.

"Hmm, let's give that another day or so shall we."

"May I ask a question?" I asked.

"You may, though I am not sure if I would be able to answer"

"My unit. Do you know anything about what happened?"

"During combat in the Netherlands? I know nothing, sorry. However, I can tell you that your orders came in a few days ago. You will be going to the eastern front as soon as we've patched you up"

I was silent. The eastern front. It meant almost certainly death.

"Not the best news, I know" he said.

"No, it's not. But, we go where we are ordered"

He leaned in, and whispered "Between you and me, Obersharführer, the casualty rates on the eastern front have been catastrophic, especially in our Waffen SS units"

"I've heard the same" I said. I had. The Leibstandarte Adolf Hitler had been in the east for a few years now, and their numbers had been decimated. One of my childhood friends, Franz, had been lucky enough to join the elite LAH unit; it had been the proudest day of his life. Then, two weeks after finishing his basic training in Berlin, his unit had been shipped out to the Ukraine.

He had been killed the day after they had arrived; shot by a sniper whilst walking to the latrine. I didn't want to go to the east, it was cold out there, really cold. And the Russians were barbarians. They tortured and mutilated captured Waffen SS soldiers.

"I'll come back and check on you in the morning, try to sleep" he said, and went off to see to his next patient.
I put thoughts of the east out of my mind. It wasn't easy. It terrified me. I lay for a long time, just staring at the ceiling, thinking about what I should do. Eventually, I lost the battle and fell into a deep sleep.

"Good morning Obersharführer"
I woke with a start. "What!?" My shout echoed around the room. I looked around, and calmed. I was still in the hospital. My dreams had been haunted by gruesome images of combat.
"You slept well I hope?" It was the nurse from yesterday, doing her morning rounds.
"Yes, yes I did" I said, focusing on the girl in front of me, instead of the images of broken bodies in my mind. She was beautiful.
"Good. How is the leg feeling?"
I moved my leg without thinking. A searing pain shot up my left side "Aaaah! Verdammt!" I shouted.
"Try not to move!" she said, hurrying to my side "You're leg hasn't healed yet. It needs rest"
I remembered to indoctrination during our basic training: "Pain is in the brain". We were trained to think pain didn't exist; that the Waffen SS man didn't feel pain, he should fight on, regardless of injury. Hmm, this pain was definitely NOT in the brain; it was very real.
"I suppose so" I laughed. "You have a moment to sit?"
"I can spare a war hero five minutes" she said, and sat.
"Can I ask you something?"
"Of course"
"First off, my name is Joseph, not Oberscharführer"
"Gisela, not nurse" she replied.
"What a beautiful name. Pleased to meet you Gisela"
Just speaking her name out loud made me feel happy.

What an effect his woman was having on me.
She blushed "Thank you. Pleased to meet you too. Your question?"
"My question" I paused "Oh, yes, my question"
"Yes?"
"I've been offered a choice of posting after I get out of here"
"That's great" she smiled "You deserve it"
"I'm not sure about that, but, the Captain mentioned transferring to a non-combat role"
"Sounds like sound advice" she said.
"Yes it does. However, leaving my comrades behind would feel like betrayal"
"I can understand that" she said "However, consider your position; would you want to end up back here again? Or worse?"
"It is what I signed up for, what I trained for. I would not dishonour myself or my parents"
"Ach, you men with your honour. You have a Knights Cross, how much more honour do you want? I'm sure your parents would prefer to be proud of their living son, rather than honouring a dead one"
"Are you always so forward in your answers?" I asked.
"Forgive me, I didn't meant to offend or be presumptuous" She hung her head.
"I was joking" I smiled "You give sound, honest advice. I thank you for it"
"Do you know where your next posting is?" she asked, smiling.
"Eastern front"
The smile disappeared instantly. "Oh"
"I know" I said.
"I hear nothing but terrible things about the east, the losses are incredibly high"
"I hear the same. But, should I let my comrades fight alone?"
"You have a choice" she said.

"Yes, I do"
"Seems like an obvious choice to me"
"How so? You think I should abandon my comrades?"
"The losses are so high, what difference would one man make?"
"Who knows? Maybe all the difference"
"Maybe none. Many brave men die out there every day" she said.
I laughed "People die everywhere, what difference would it make where I am?"
She was not amused "Do you want to die?" She looked angry, it made me feel bad.
"Of course not. But my comrades..."
She cut me off "Your comrades will do just as well without you. Don't be a fool"
"You wouldn't know what I mean" I said, dismissively. This angered her.
"Oh really? And why not? You think I don't see the broken men they send here from the front every day? The hospital is full of men with the most horrendous injuries. I'm surrounded by death and suffering. You think the parents of the dead are happy that their sons died for our country? With honour? No, they are devastated that the boy they spent years raising and nurturing is gone."
"I'm sorry" I said "I didn't mean to offend"
She breathed deeply "No, it is I who is sorry, I shouldn't have snapped at you. I just see so much suffering" she started crying. My god man, look at what you've done. I scolded myself. Fool. She was right; what difference would one man make? Did I really want to die? Did I want to break my mother's heart?
"Snow isn't really my thing" I said.
"What?" she looked up.
"I don't do well in the cold" I added.
"You have decided then?" she asked, wiping her eyes.
"I have"

A beautiful smile spread across her face.
I reached for the slip of paper "I will need a telephone"

Loyalty and Honour is available on Amazon now!

Printed in Great Britain
by Amazon